Working-class and anarchisn.

Debates and polemics from Workers' Liberty and *Solidarity*

Third edition, September 2012

Phoenix Press 2012
ISBN 978-0-9531864-6-4

Phoenix Press
Workers' Liberty
20E Tower Workshops
Riley Road
London SE1 3DG

Contents

This pamphlet is a collection of articles and speeches discussing the AWL and the politics of anarchism, by both members and non-members of the AWL. Most of the texts appeared in the AWL newspaper *Solidarity*, some in edited or abridged forms. Some of the texts are extracted from lengthy online debates which we could not reprint in full. For each text, a URL is given where longer exchanges may be found.

An open letter to a direct-action militant

By Ira Berkovic

Solidarity 199, 30 March 2011. This open letter was written as a contribution to a debate that ensued following direct actions taken by activists attending the TUC-organised "March for the Alternative" on 26 March 2011, the biggest trade union demonstration in British history.

URL: bit.ly/h0lHYN

Comrade,

We are sympathetic to the direct action taken against banks, Fortnum & Mason, the Ritz Hotel and other locations throughout central London on Saturday 26 March. We will not join in with moralistic condemnations of your "violence", nor will we go along with attempts to "disown" you or pretend you are not part of our movement. Indeed, some Workers' Liberty members were involved in the direct actions which took place on Saturday.

We will not join in with attempts in the media and elsewhere to create a division between respectable, non-violent direct-action activists and "bad", troublemaking "anarchists".

We share many of your instincts; you have our sympathy, our solidarity against any police repression.

Like you, we see the conservatism of the labour movement leaders as an obstacle. Like you, we know that the working-class anti-cuts movement will need more creative tactics than "A to B" marches followed by long rallies if we are seriously to threaten this government. And, like you, we think that places like the Ritz Hotel and Fortnum & Mason — symbols of the opulent luxury the rich continue to enjoy while we lose our jobs, homes and services — are legitimate targets for symbolic direct action.

But we also think that such action is only symbolic. Symbolic actions have their place, but they are not enough. A mere proliferation of symbolic action, counterposed to traditional demonstrations, will not in itself give us the movement we need. To get that movement we will need a serious political campaign to build it, the frontline of which will not be in the exciting and dangerous cut-and-thrust of a ruckus with the cops but in the day-to-day lives of our fellow workers in workplaces and communities.

We think there's a problem with the way in which direct actions of the kind undertaken on Saturday can create unnecessary and unhelpful, even hierarchical, divisions between the mass labour movement and direct-action activists. If activists meet in secret, have special direct-action "skills", and undertake their actions without any accountability to mass labour movement organisations they risk becoming an "elite". Wouldn't it be better to organise direct actions which took with them, or had the sympathy of, sizeable sections of the main movement against cuts?

The labour movement is frequently a politically dull and conservative place to spend your time. Smashing up some ostentatious symbols of capitalist excess certainly makes a more immediate impact than plugging away within most trade union branches to democratise and radicalise them, and it usually feels a lot better, too.

But means condition ends, and if your end goal is a mass, class-based movement capable of mobilising not just seasoned direct-action veterans but hundreds of thousands of ordinary workers (the sort of people who, for the most part, stuck to the main route of the march on Saturday and probably wouldn't have known how to get involved in the direct actions even if they'd wanted to), then means other than taking those actions in a unilateral and unaccountable way will be necessary.

We believe that many of the people who see radical direct action as a primary focus (some of whom identify as anarchists) share with us some form of class politics; you believe that the working class is the social force capable of changing the world. If that's true, we think you should consider what relationship your activism has to the organised movement of that class — however politically inadequate its leadership may currently be.

The labour movement needs your energy and innovation. For want of better words, it needs your "courage" and daring. The size of Saturday's demonstration shows us that we could now be entering a period where mass action of working-class people becomes a more viable possibility. This means we need to be creative and innovative and come up with direct-action tactics that are accessible to the "mass" of people and are not the exclusive property of those with the skills to undertake them. To develop those tactics, the dynamism and creativity of the direct-action movement and of activists like you will be needed.

But, conversely, you "need" the labour movement. Your revolutionary

5

anti-capitalist instincts cannot become a political reality without an agency capable of giving them meaningful content. That agency is the working class.

This doesn't mean that it's only legitimate to take radical direct action if some labour movement body sanctions it or if there's a critical mass of workers taking part. But it does mean that without mass working-class direct actions, symbolic direct actions can ultimately only serve to create direct-action "elites" and provide ammunition to the right wing and the state.

Our aim is a movement of workers capable of taking over shops, banks and other buildings — not just smashing them up.

If you want to build that movement too, direct-action organising is at best limited and inadequate. You should become — or, if you are already, more consistently see yourself as — a labour-movement activist.

Can we build a revolutionary workers' movement?

By Ira Berkovic

Solidarity 200, 6 April 2011

URL: bit.ly/jc97HE

Argument: trade unions are a spent force. They're half the size they were in the 1970s; most workers know little about trade unions, if they've even heard of them at all. By focusing your activism on the labour movement and rooting it in trade unions, you're cutting yourself off from the majority of working-class people.

It's true that trade unions have suffered historic defeats over the past generation which have diminished their size and power. The decisive defeat suffered in the mid-1980s, when Thatcher succeeded in defeating the miners' strike, broke the back of the labour movement. It has yet to recover. But why assume that defeat is permanent, and then abandon the political terrain of the labour movement to the sell-out bureaucrats who currently lead it?

For us, rooting our activism in the trade union movement is not about whether the movement in a given period is stronger or weaker, or whether it has more or less members. Trade unions represent something unique and "special" as social and political forms under capitalism. They're not alien organisations implanted in society by some outside force; they are the basic self-defence organisations that workers have always created throughout the history of capitalism. They are an inevitable, organic product of class struggle. In some ways they are a concrete, organisational manifestation of that struggle. They organise workers, as workers, at the point of exploitation in workplaces.

That's not to say that class struggle only takes place at work, or that only currently-employed workers can participate in class struggle, or that capitalist society does not breed other oppressions (such as gender and racial oppression). But the nucleus of capitalism is the exploitation of wage-labour by bosses. Workplaces — and the self-created organisations which organically emerge in workplaces — are a key site for building and shaping anti-capitalist struggles.

7

The class-struggle experiences that we experience at work are different from our class-struggle experiences elsewhere. We can form tenants' associations or claimants' groups to fight class battles around issues like housing and welfare, but it's only at work that we're in a position to organise collectively with our fellow workers to not only disrupt but actually take control of production. Workplaces are capitalism's engine room, and that means the relationships which exist there and the organisations which emerge are particularly important.

We do not think that existing trade-union organisations are adequate in terms of revolutionary class struggle. We don't even think they're adequate for fighting for basic reforms within the framework of capitalism. Within our focus on the labour movement, we fight for very different forms of trade-union organisation — more democratic, more militant, more expansive. We also believe in the need for political organisations for revolutionary workers. But none of that can be built by "going around" the only movement in which workers are currently organised as workers and which still has between six and seven million members. As such it is the only real mass movement in British society.

Some comrades, including some anarchist comrades — those who believe in class politics and want to see a militant workers' movement — seem to want to build a revolutionary workers' movement from scratch. Perhaps they think that our approach of revolutionising the existing movement will take too long and is too hard. It will certainly take time, and it will certainly not be easy. But, compared to the goal of building a revolutionary workers' movement from scratch that "short-cuts" around the organisations, experiences, history and consciousness of the existing mass labour movement, it is infinitely more possible as well as more necessary.

Trade unions are controlled at every level by the worst kind of sell-outs and bureaucrats. Reactionary attitudes about race, gender and sexuality are still rife within many trade unions and many trade union officials are more interested in maintaining their own position than helping their members organise. The so-called "political wing" of the labour movement, the Labour Party, is led by insipid careerists who'd make pretty much the same cuts the Tories are making.

All true. But if you want the situation to be different, how does it make sense to allow such people's control of the movement to continue unchallenged?

Again, the relatively better or worse politics of labour-movement leaders has never been the reason for working-class revolutionaries to focus their activism in the labour movement. It's because of the organic relationship of trade unions to the class struggle.

The history of the labour movement is full of examples of ordinary workers, trade union members, organising together to wrest control of their unions from bureaucrats and reactionaries in the most adverse conditions imaginable.

Rank-and-file networks like the US Teamsters for a Democratic Union even took on the power of organised crime to fight for greater militancy and member-leadership in their union. Democracy activists in the United Mine Workers of America had to contend with their candidate for the union presidency in 1969 being assassinated by the union's leadership.

Activists in Britain don't face similar dangers. What stands in our way is the inertia and demoralisation instilled in us by so many years of defeat. But small sparks can light big fires. Already, the student mobilisations of November-December 2010 have inspired significant numbers of workers. Many trade unionists are asking why there aren't activist networks within their movement capable of organising actions on a similar scale. That's a question that will bring them into conflict with their own leaderships and bureaucracies.

If the "direct-action activists" (for want of a better term) who currently don't see the labour movement as a focus for their activism and organising were to turn their energies towards building up grassroots networks inside and across trade unions that could challenge the power of the kind of people we heard speak on the Hyde Park platform of the "March for the Alternative", a world of possibilities opens up.

Sometimes, struggles to transform trade unions begin as seemingly small-scale battles over very day-to-day issues. The grassroots network that eventually took over and revolutionised the New South Wales Builders' Labourers Federation in Australia in the 1970s first came together to campaign around basic health-and-safety issues on building sites. Workers developed skills and ideas by fighting on the "bread-and-butter" issues, and built up the confidence to then go after the bigger issues too — for example, they fought important environmental battles.

Trade unions only organise in particular workplaces. The most vulnerable and exploited members of the working class — migrant workers, precarious workers and workers employed by high-street corporations like McDonalds and Starbucks — are largely ignored by the trade unions or dismissed as "too hard" to organise.

It doesn't have to be like this. The history of the trade union movement internationally, both recent and more distant, proves it.

Britain's big general unions — GMB and Unite — trace their origins to the "New Unionism" of the late 19th century. These were a series of struggles, led mainly by revolutionary socialists, to organise workers such as dockers and gasworkers — the semi-skilled, precarious and often migrant workers frequently ignored by the old, conservative "craft" unions. New Unionism organised workers on a militant basis, in contrast to the conciliatory approach of the older craft unions, and won significant victories.

And more recently? In 2006, the small New Zealand union Unite launched a campaign to organise workers working for employers such as McDonalds, Pizza Hut, Starbucks and KFC. These workers were overwhelmingly young and had had little or no contact with trade unions before.

Unite organised on a democratic basis and took on the power of notoriously anti-union corporations that bigger, more established unions had been too timid and conservative to confront.

The Supersize My Pay campaign that Unite ran succeeded in securing the abolition of the discriminatory youth rates of the New Zealand minimum wage, amounting to a serious wage increase for thousands of workers.

The dynamism of the campaign also shook up the rest of the New Zealand labour movement. Unite was affiliated to the NZCTU (the New Zealand equivalent of the TUC) and saw itself as part of an attempt to radicalise trade-union politics across the country, not as a breakaway attempting to build an alternative movement outside of the existing one.

Although the experiences of New Unionism and Supersize My Pay are separated by history, geography and scale, they both prove that hyperexploited workers can and do organise. The experiences of sweatshop workers from Haiti to Mexico to Indonesia who have taken on their bosses and won prove the same. The more activists believing in the politics and spirit of struggles like New Unionism and Supersize My Pay active in the mainstream labour movement, the greater the chance of building a New Unionism in 21st century Britain.

What New Unionism and Supersize My Pay also have in common is the central role of a dedicated core of revolutionary socialist activists. The role of Marxists such as Eleanor Marx, Tom Mann, Ben Tillett, Will Thorne and John Burns to New Unionism was crucial in the 1880s and 90s.

Supersize My Pay happened in part because a group of New Zealand socialists made a conscious decision to dedicate themselves to the work of building it.

The lesson for us today is twofold. First, it shows that political organisation is necessary to help clarify ideas, build bonds of solidarity between activists and help us educate and train each other. Second, it shows that a group of anti-capitalist revolutionaries who decide to commit to the long, hard struggle of transforming the labour movement can have an enormous impact.

You say strikes are a more effective form of direct action than taking action against banks or shops, but strikes rarely win anything. London Underground workers, supposedly the most powerful group of workers in the country, recently took four days of strike action against cuts and won absolutely nothing.

Strikes are rarely successful in Britain today because the unions — including the supposedly more militant ones led by non-revolutionary leftists and Stalinists — have developed a culture in which strikes are not really strikes, but incidental exercises in chest-beating; abstract expressions of protest and letting-off-steam.

Even in the "militant unions" like the PCS and RMT, strikes usually happen for one day only and with little or no strategy for using workers' industrial strength to force concessions from management. Picket lines don't function as picket lines; in most places strike-breakers are allowed to walk past with little but a disapproving tut or two from their workmates.

That culture needs to change. But even despite this, it's not true that strikes never win anything.

Where workers have taken higher-impact or escalated action recently, they have won victories. The indefinite strike at Tower Hamlets College in autumn 2009 was partially successful and the sit-down strikes (occupations) at Ford Visteon and Vestas also secured some concessions.

The 2006 pensions dispute, the single-biggest piece of industrial action in the UK since the 1926 general strike, forced the government to change (partially) its plans for pension reforms. Looking abroad, the mass stu-

11

dent-worker strike movement of 2006 in France forced Jacques Chirac to scrap his new labour law (the CPE) even after it had been passed by parliament.

All of these campaigns involved radical, imaginative and daring direct actions — but they were actions that were linked to, and carried out in solidarity with, workplace-based direct action taken by workers.

To imagine that, because most bosses and the state are capable of riding out the odd day or two of strike action, strikes are a less effective form of direct action than the actions we saw on the edges of the "March for the Alternative" is to miss the point about how capitalism functions. Our understanding about the fundamental mechanisms at the heart of capitalism has to be our guide.

What makes the capitalist class shift its perspective (to make concessions or to strike back at us) isn't stopping the shopping at Fortnum & Mason or getting Philip Green to pay his taxes. What bothers capitalists most is workers withdrawing their labour power — when workers do it enough, and over a sustained period of time, it bothers capitalists a lot.

That is not to say that direct actions against Fortnum & Mason etc are illegitimate or pointless; far from it. But if our goal is disrupting and ultimately overthrowing capitalist class relations then our primary focus has to be on building the kind of direct action best placed to do that: strikes.

The mini-wave of 2009 has put radical industrial direct action such as indefinite strikes and workplace occupations back on the agenda for labour movement activists. These actions pose the question of power much more sharply than any number of paintbombs thrown at any number of banks.

Your task of revolutionising the existing labour movement could take generations. In unions like Unison, it's incredibly difficult to get the bureaucracy to sanction strike ballots. We can't wait that long; we need to take action that will make bosses and the state sit up and listen now. Passing radical motions in the odd union branch or Trades Council won't make them do that, but radical direct action against the corporate property they care about might.

Yes, it might. And Workers' Liberty has never said that direct action of that kind is illegitimate. Far from it. Our members support and have been involved in UK Uncut-type actions and our student members were at the forefront of the Millbank protests in November 2010.

There is not necessarily a counterposition between sometimes organising or being involved in actions of that kind and the longer-term project of revolutionising the existing labour movement. In fact, the two things can have a symbiotic relationship.

Millbank did have an impact on the political culture inside the trade union movement.

Every picket line that took place in the aftermath of the student movement was full of conversations about what the students had done and whether the trade unions could ever do something similar.

The debate is about where our activism should be fundamentally rooted and what we see as the means which can achieve our ends. If our end goal is working-class self-emancipation, then our focus must necessarily be on helping our class organise. For that, there can be no shortcut around the existing organisations organically and inevitably generated by class struggle. Focusing elsewhere may be easier. It may be more exhilarating. In the short-term it may have more impact. But it will not — it cannot — serve the goal of working-class self-emancipation in anything other than a limited and symbolic way.

In part, it comes down to a question of whether we simply want to give the capitalists — or rather, some capitalists — a bloody nose from time to time or whether we want to overthrow and replace their entire system. That latter goal cannot be achieved merely by an accumulation of spectacular, symbolic acts. It is a lengthy process, and one which will involve going through, and learning from, the experience of losing before we eventually win. As the American socialist Hal Draper, quoting Rosa Luxemburg, put it, "the socialist revolution is necessarily a continuous series of defeats, followed by only one victory." If we are serious revolutionaries we should commit to going through those experiences, learning political lessons from those experiences, as part of our class, for as long as it takes.

We believe that many of the activists who are ostensibly on the "other side" of this debate from us are probably much closer to us politically than most of the self-proclaimed "Trotskyist" left with whom we notionally share a tradition. That is why we want to understand and engage with the reasons why so many young activists do not see the labour movement as a necessary political focus. We believe that if we can combine the energy, dynamism, innovation and indeed the militant anger represented by the best of the "direct-action" movement with a consistent focus on working-class organising and a long-term struggle to revolutionise the labour movement, then something like New Unionism

13

becomes possible again.

The New South Wales BLF becomes possible again. The CPE movement becomes possible again. Supersize My Pay becomes possible again. And, ultimately, working-class revolution becomes possible again.

Ends and means: continuing the debate on tactics

By Anne Archist

April 2011. Anne Archist is an activist who contributes to the Great Unrest blog (thegreatunrest.net). This article was written as a contribution to the debate in response to Ira Berkovic's "Open letter", and an edited version of it appeared in *Solidarity* 201, 11 May 2011.

URL: bit.ly/shCImj

The relationship between our political goals and the means we use to achieve them is fraught with difficulty, and there's good evidence of this in the recent debates about "direct action" and the "black bloc" (which has largely been conflated with the act of rioting itself).

On the one hand, we can fixate on one particular way of doing things to the exclusion of better possibilities; on the other hand, we can valorise "diversity of tactics" as if it were an end in itself. When people have forgotten what should be self-evident truths it's often necessary to straighten them out by reminding them of seemingly banal ways of looking at the topic.

With that in mind, we need to stop thinking in terms of tactics as a singular — or else infinitely diverse — way of achieving a singular goal. The left needs to incorporate appropriate tactics depending on the challenge that we face in a particular situation. We need to ensure that our line of march on one front doesn't contradict our line of march on another front. Activists need to think in terms of winning immediate struggles and in terms of their long-term political objectives (be they bringing down the current government, ensuring socialist revolution, smashing the state, or whatever).

All of this should hopefully mean more dialogue about ends, rather than the recent fixation on means. I get the impression that a lot of political friction derives from a misunderstanding of the relationship between means and ends and the nature of those means and ends.

Take the example of good-hearted workers or students who ask class-struggle militants why they don't take up a career in politics; the naïve assumption is that the official political channels can be turned to whatever ends one would desire, that they don't contain built-in biases and limitations. The question sounds faintly absurd to those of us who think that the problems of British politics are systemic and class-based, and that the state serves largely to further the interests of the capitalist class, because it is this perspective that reveals the misfit between intentions and methods in this instance.

The problem is to explain our political objectives in the long and short term, and our understanding of the relationship between different available means and the ends we seek, to those who don't share our perspective in the anti-cuts movement, the student movement, or whatever. It would be fair to say that the AWL have a good record on this relationship (and I speak as a non-member), and they're not the only political organisation who do, but I don't want to encourage complacency or let other Marxist groups off easily.

This puts us on a better footing to critique each other as comrades, serves us in setting reformists straight when we enter into dialogue them, allows a better grasp of our strategy and tactics to the people we work with in broader coalitions, and finally forces us to come to grips with a relationship that is important even just for the sake of us developing the right approach and realistically assessing our ideas.

You have to wonder, for instance, if other left groups would be as keen to fetishise general strikes if they had to explain how a one-day stoppage in the public sector would relate to stopping the cuts, bringing down the government, or whatever it is they seem to think this would be an integral part of — could it be detrimental to this goal if it was a flop, for instance?

Anarchism, direct action and class struggle: a reply to Ira Berkovic's "Open letter"

By Bobi Pasquale

Solidarity 202, 4 May 2011

URL: bit.ly/t9Z3nV

"A riot is the language of the unheard" (Martin Luther King)

Currently [the phrase] "direct action" seems to be used mechanically for any action outside the once standard, ignored, tedious and silent marches.

There is an important differentiation between vandalism and violence — neither of which ought necessarily be condemned — but the argument differs slightly.

On the question of direct action — occupations, strikes, civil disobedience and yes, sometimes property damage —I find it difficult to comprehend the arguments against this method to stop cuts that will rocket up child poverty, homelessness, unemployment and severely threaten many students' access to education.

Many, and rightly so, are furious about the coalition's plans and in actuality, who suffers the greater cost? The multi-billionaire capitalist who needs to replace his window, or the 15 year old who has lost all their EMA and is expected to pay £27,000 plus for a degree?

Who is the violent perpetrator? The student who refuses to be bullied and stands shoulder to shoulder with everyone fighting for the same cause; or the armoured policeman who clubs children and hospitalises people refusing to accept injustice?

Who is the threat? The masked student, or the police; hard hats, shields, batons, cuffs?

Those who retaliate "policemen are just workers in uniform" or "they're just doing their job": contemplate this... Ian Tomlinson. Smiley Culture. Jean Charles de Menezes. Kingsley Brown.

The police have proven time and time again, they do not protect us. They protect the richest, whitest politicians of the world and breed murderers rarely brought to trial. Do not swallow the lies of the papers declaring the police to be innocently containing a violent mob.

If you don't believe us, join us on a demonstration and when you find yourself nose to nose with a baton; you may stop condemning us.

One need only look closer at those who condemn us. Careerist, Labour wannabes who slip through the crowds whilst we are hit, and drink tea with MPs and negotiate their futures.

Really though, we can be the threat. Direct actions requires mass participation to be truly effective. Ultimately we are the majority, and working together, we can become ungovernable. We didn't even vote for this despicable Government. When we are imprisoned, beaten and continuously oppressed by a state clearly against us — we must fight back. Direct action is a key way to do this.

Most groups are not focused on smashing windows. The smashing usually occurs after police provocation or as a result of other methods. For example, Millbank windows were initially smashed as a part of the occupation.

Occupations are important as they empower individuals and groups to reclaim the spaces that belong to us. Money is the only language capitalists understand; so when we occupy their department stores (Fortnum & Masons, Vodafone etc), we shut down their business, and they lose profit. We also bring solidarity between groups and enable communication and conversation between those to be hit by the cuts.

When the workers strike, they stop production, and stop the work the government continuously exploits. To build a successful movement we must stand in absolute solidarity with these workers. Some forms of industrial action such as wildcat strikes, go-slows etc workers can engage in without relying on official union approval.

Yet again, the most underrepresented, oppressed communities of our society are hardest hurt by the cuts — black and LGBT communities, and women. We would not condemn the direct action of the suffragettes who often ran with the motto of "deeds, not words" and were regularly imprisoned and slandered. Fighting the cuts is a question of liberation. Liberation from capitalist exploitation; and for this goal and emancipation, spraying "Fight Sexism" on Anne Summers is a tiny part of a wider movement, and justified.

However many bureaucrats, who supposedly represent us, concentrate far too much on pen pushing and pointless negotiation rather than allowing us to self organise and make decisions amongst ourselves. Strikes for example are often at the expense of leaders agreeing to it. Whilst many socialists call for a general strike, they do not seem to understand that this is only possible by overpowering the so-called representative structures, including in their much loved unions. As Emma Goldman said; "Organisation, as we understand it, however, is a different thing. It is based, primarily, on freedom. It is a natural and voluntary grouping of energies to secure results beneficial to humanity."

Unions are often based in an HQ distant from the actual workplace. Their leaders are paid a significant wage, and they are often hijacked by careerists or patronising academics who think they have an authority to speak on behalf of their members.

Actually, they are probably on sabbatical and no longer do the same work as everybody else, and spend more time in meetings negotiating with managements, than on the ground empowering the workers. To cite the current unions as the only way for the movement is simplistic and not viable.

For AWL to publish such incorrect articles such as "Open letter to a direct-action militant" (*Solidarity* 200), is insulting but also laughable. To talk of anarchists (and let's be clear, the article is clearly aimed at anarchists), as elite, unhelpful and merely symbolic is concerning.

"Smashing up some ostentatious symbols of capitalist excess certainly makes a more immediate impact than plugging away within most trade union branches to democratise and radicalise them."

Firstly, the author has clearly failed to read SolFed's open letter to UK Uncut, http://bit.ly/hSp3Jp. This article directly states that we must go further in our direct action, whilst not condemning action taken.

Secondly, whilst many anarchists openly criticise the roles and structures of the union, socialists are often merely reformist. Reformism is inevitably going to fail as Emma Goldman clearly puts it; "Good men, if such there be, would either remain true to their political faith and lose their economic support, or they would cling to their economic master and be utterly unable to do the slightest good". This is applicable to overtaking any institutions currently failing to support us.

Further, anarchists recognise the limitations of unions, the bureaucracy and in-fighting that is detrimental to the organisation and action of its membership. Indeed, any dictating is oppressive, whether well intentioned or not.

The author of the AWL piece even recognises this; "The labour movement is frequently a politically dull and conservative place to spend your time." So why not use that time to create a labour movement of accessible, transparent and self-organised groupings, to enable us to respond to these cuts as effectively as possible and in genuine solidarity. "But, conversely, you 'need' the labour movement. Your revolutionary anti-capitalist instincts cannot become a political reality without an agency capable of giving them meaningful content. That agency is the working class." What anarcho-syndicalist is dismissive of the working class? This does not make any sense and is highly patronising.

The working class is not the same as Leninist tactics. If anything, it is anarchism that militantly supports a mass movement of the working class and reclaims the power.

"You should become — or, if you are already, more consistently see yourself as — a labour-movement activist". This too is utterly dismissive of the fact that most anarchists are labour activists, whose priorities lay differently to the repetitive aim of moving through elected positions.

Direct action is a necessary tactic that enables individuals to be at the forefront of their own movement, to make mass decisions in a safe space without being dictated to by a political party of any persuasion, and to ultimately, fight back against a cutting coalition government which exploits us, cheats us and lies to us. Anarchism is a tool to do this, despite the slanderous propaganda of most, on all sides.

Direct action and class struggle: a reply to Bobi Pasquale

By Sacha Ismail

Solidarity 203, 11 May 2011

URL: bit.ly/TrkI8G

Much of Bobi Pasquale's response to our "Open letter to a direct action militant" (*Solidarity* 202) was made up of statements no leftist could object to (workers and students in struggle good; the cuts, coppers and Labour careerists bad).

And while the Socialist Party, for instance, believes the police are "workers in uniform", and has as its "priority" in the labour movement "moving through elected positions" — these are certainly not accusations you can make at the AWL. They are not relevant to this debate.

I'd urge everyone interested in this debate to read "Can we build a revolutionary workers' movement?", published in *Solidarity* in April, which discusses some of these issues at length. If Bobi had read it, she would not necessarily have been persuaded, but she might have engaged with our actual arguments a bit more.

What are the real disagreements?

1. Judging by what she writes here, I think Bobi fetishises direct action as such, essentially detaching it from class struggle. We should certainly support direct action by many different groups and social forces, but it is not necessarily the same thing as direct action by the working class, at the point of production and beyond that in a class movement whose base is the organisation of workers in production.

The point about a strike is not so much that it is the most effective way of making bosses lose money; what is crucial is the growth of workers' class organisation, class consciousness and ability to struggle as part of a class.

In her conclusion, what Bobi effectively counterposes to the notion of a class movement is "direct action [as] a tactic that enables individuals to be at the forefront of their own movement, to make mass decisions in a safe space..." Class and class struggle are blurred out almost completely.

On the other hand, direct action is only one element of working-class struggle, which takes place on many levels (direct action, organisation, representation; industrial, political, ideological). Direct action is not all the labour movement needs to do to organise workers and fight the bosses effectively. Supporting localised direct action by groups of workers, as Bobi urges, is far from the be all and end all of developing working-class struggle.

2. Bobi's piece reads as if she wants to start a new labour movement from scratch, instead of transforming the one we have. She does not state clearly whether she rejects completely working in bourgeois, bureaucratised trade unions, but that seems to be implied.

Without organising to resist its exploitation at the point of production, the working class would "be degraded to one level mass of broken wretches, past salvation" — and thus "certainly disqualify themselves for the initiating of any larger movement" (Marx).

Like it or not, this resistance has, across the world, consistently taken the form of organising trade unions. Unions are not the whole working-class movement, and Marxists have explained why they cannot, by themselves, overthrow capitalism (ironically, this is one of our objections to syndicalism). Their bureaucratisation is not an accident, but an inherent tendency which has to be combated. Nonetheless, they are the core, the bedrock of the workers' movement as it exists, certainly in Britain. Any talk of "class struggle" without seeking to transform them is playing around with words.

Leave aside whether most self-defined anarchists take part in anything which could meaningfully be called class-struggle activity. Even members of organised anarchist groups (AFed, SolFed) which define as class-struggle anarchist or anarcho-syndicalist are mostly either hostile to working in the unions or do not see transforming them as a strategic task. We do.

Lastly, it is not clear whether Bobi opposes large-scale (national, international), structured organisations like unions as such — implied by her apparent hostility to the whole concept of "representation". In which case, how will we have workers' councils, which involve workers electing... representatives?

3. Bobi's argument also blurs out the question of politics, and the battle of ideas. One example she cites in passing illustrates this. She praises the direct action of the suffragettes (by the way, does this mean that she doesn't share the usual anarchist objection to voting in bourgeois elections?) — but says nothing of the divisions which opened up in the suffragette movement immediately before, during and after the First World

War. This split, which led to the expulsion of the working-class suffrage movement of East London, was not along the lines of willingness to take direct action or degree of 'militancy' (what could be more 'militant' than the bourgeois suffragettes' small-scale terrorism?) It was along the class/political axes of universal suffrage vs votes for rich women; class politics vs bourgeois feminism; and democratic mass mobilisation vs authoritarian elitism.

Politics matters — direct action by whom, organised how and for what goals?

How to organise to change the world

By Ed Maltby

This is the text of a speech given by Workers' Liberty member Ed Maltby at a public debate with blogger Laurie Penny (pennyred.blogspot.com) at the University of London Union on 27 January 2011. The title of the debate was "What kind of 'new politics'?" In the course of the student and youth upheaval of November-December 2010, Laurie had written a number of high-profile articles criticising the "old left" and calling for a "new politics". In the course of the debate she described herself as "an anarchist".

URL: bit.ly/f4BVZB

Our starting point is that revolution is possible. We think that the working class — and only the working class — is capable of over-throwing capitalism and replacing it with something better. Students, people from different class backgrounds, and from different campaigns can have a role to play in this process but as auxiliaries to the working class.

It's this central belief that conditions my view of revolutionary organisation. If you think that the working class is incapable of making a revolution, or that capitalism is the best form of society possible, then none of what I am about to say will make sense to you.

We live in a capitalist world. Capitalism is not the only source of oppression — patriarchal and religious oppressions persist which pre-date capitalism — but capitalism, the rule of profit, is responsible for most of the cruelties and absurdities of the way our world is organised: war, hunger, environmental destruction and all the rest: it comes from the exploitation of class by class.

The mainspring of capitalism is the exploitation of wage labour by capitalists. And because of this, the working class, the class which has its hands on the wheels of production, the class which is taught by capitalism how to co-operate on a global scale in order to operate the machinery of capitalist society; they can overthrow this system, re-organise society on the basis of common ownership, and social need, not profit.

This class has no class beneath it to exploit. It owns nothing. Collective ownership of the means of production is the only way that the working class can rule in its own name and in its own interests. The only way for a mass of people to own anything collectively is through mass democracy. And that means that the working class must take power consciously. It must understand what it is doing. Millions of workers must understand the process of revolution, and choose it, and debate it publicly. A cadre of experts cannot do it on their behalf, or it's not a revolution. It cannot happen gradually, or by accident. A democratic working-class movement must consciously decide to seize power, together, and do it. Otherwise the workers will not be liberating themselves.

In order to do this, the working class needs a way of coming together, to debate, to consider the experience of struggle, to educate itself and develop revolutionary ideas. Under a constant barrage of capitalist propaganda and pressure from cradle to grave, this cannot be done by workers individually. It needs to be a collective effort.

So why a party, and not just a sort of revolutionary think-tank churning out ideas? Firstly, because think-tank-type bodies are not democratic or collective, really. You need not just a collection of individuals writing papers — you need those ideas to be the property of everyone in the organisation, collectively worked on, debated — and put into practice.

Secondly, an organisation needs not only to talk about ideas, but it needs to organise, teaching through struggle, intervening in all the clashes between workers and bosses, small and large, to increase the confidence and self-activity of the workers around the organisation. A party like this is not like a typical bourgeois party, or a Stalinist party, which has an active leadership and a passive membership or voter base. A revolutionary workers' organisation needs to break down the division between leaders and led, to create a struggling collective of equals. This is a minority, sure — but it's a minority trying constantly to raise the rest of the workers to its own level, through struggle.

It's true that sometimes, during a great upsurge in struggle, miracles happen. In a small way, we have seen this with the student movement, which came out of nowhere. All of a sudden, thousands of people were thrown into activity and suddenly received a political education which the existing left organisations couldn't have given them. They were able to improvise an impressive movement, quickly. But an understanding of capitalist society, an understanding of the history of working-class struggle, in short, the idea that revolution is needed — these things can't be improvised or thrown together at the last minute. And these things determine the fate of a sudden upsurge in struggle — who does the movement look to for political direction? Who do they look to, to answer the question, "what next?" What are the ideas that guide the movement? If activists haven't been armed with Marxist ideas in advance, other ideas, sometimes useless ones, sometimes plain reactionary ones, can fill the void.

Also, thousands of workers can't be taken through an experience of struggle at will. You can't wish a general strike into being, and it is very hard to tell when one will take place. The lessons of past struggles need to be remembered and transmitted from one generation to the next. You can't expect these educational experiences to be renewed so regularly. After a big defeat, there can follow a long lull, during which lessons learned from the last upsurge can be forgotten, or their meaning corrupted. This current movement will also recede, its lessons will also be forgotten — unless they are preserved by a conscious effort by a stable group.

At this point, it's important to note that a lot of people are disgusted by the idea of a Leninist, revolutionary party. This has got to do with people's experience of how most of the so-called Leninist organisations in existence today operate. There will be some people in the room tonight who have been chewed up and spat out by the internal regimes of some of these groups. It doesn't help that most of these organisations describe themselves as Trotskyist — when they have inherited ways of thinking, organising and debating which come directly from Stalinism. I don't intend to defend these organisations. I think people are right to mistrust them. In Workers' Liberty, we are for a new politics. We want to establish a culture on the left that's free of these traits. One of the things we want our group to do is function as a power hose to clean this crap off the left. But it's important to look at exactly what these traits are.

1) Undemocratic internal regimes.

Put simply, in many organisations on the left, members are prevented from meaningfully debating or questioning their party's line. The pages of most leftwing newspapers don't contain debate: only the official line is presented. If there is any discussion of a given topic within the ranks of the party, it is not presented in the paper. That means that the paper can't function as a tool for the movement to hash out ideas — or as an effective memory bank for the class. In most left groups, factions are banned or subject to ridiculous bureaucratic restrictions. But factional struggle — organising collectively to change your comrades' minds on a given idea — that's the mechanism through which an organisation thinks!

Many people in this room will personally know people who have been

26

expelled from the SWP for the crime of "factionalism" — the idea that factions should be banned is ludicrous!

This is related to

2) Saying the line, instead of what you think

A few years ago, there was a split in the socialist group Workers' Power, over the world economy and perspectives in Britain. The group pretty much split down the middle. A huge fight was going on over a crucial question. But no-one outside their organisation knew about the disagreement inside the organisation until it had already happened. Their incredibly strict rules governing debate meant that the argument had to take place in secret. This means that not only did their public press not carry anything about what all members of the group presumably thought was an extremely important political issue — but in conversations, members had to pretend that no disagreement existed! The culture of the group, if not the rulebook, obliged members to say the opposite of what they thought.

This culture, which bureaucratically controls arguments, is dominant on the left. It teaches people that open disagreement can only ever be hostile, or "sectarian". It teaches people that the theory of a group has to be the property of experts on the central committee, and it is not anyone else's business to seriously question it. It criminalises dissent within the group. Reason is replaced by bureaucratic manoeuvre. This is not a way of teaching people to emancipate themselves. It's not an effective way of understanding reality. It is chemically pure Stalinism and we have to ditch it.

3) The party as an end in itself

The root of a lot of these maladies is the idea that the party itself, rather than the working class, will carry out the revolution. A lot of so-called Leninists have the idea of the party as a kind of army, which will organise a lot of people around one will, and this army will carry out the revolution. We don't think that. We don't think that. Revolution will be a conscious act of working-class self-emancipation or it will not be a revolution.

We don't see "the revolutionary party" as a monolithic machine which must simply be built slavishly until it is big enough to seize power. We see revolutionary parties — and undoubtedly in any revolutionary upsurge there would be more than one — as democratic collectives of revolutionary workers that seek to agitate, educate and organise. A revolutionary party is an organised political tendency within the working class seeking to convince the majority of its ideas; it is not an external force seeking to "lead" the working class like some kind of army.

We think that the basis of mass revolutionary movements has to be feeling and political conviction. A party committee cannot produce a revolution to order, and party cadres can't carry out themselves. But a lot of groups, like the SWP, seem to think that this is the case. SWP activists have a stock speech about the need for the revolutionary party. They say, "the bourgeoisie is very organised, and we need to be very organised too. That's why we need a party".

It's true that we need to be organised. But we need ideas, too! The SWP, with their ban on serious internal discussion, the sacredness of the Central Committee line, view the party not as a debater, an educator and a persuader: they view it as an apparatus, which projects instructions and disciplines the activity of the movement: "It doesn't matter what you think, all these debates are boring — go and hand out these leaflets!" But this is not a project for self-emancipation. This is a project for building an organisation for its own sake.

4) Finally, when you get into this state of mind — when you think that the party is the only entity that matters, and it is by the disciplined action of the party alone that the revolution will be brought about, then you become disconnected from the basic spirit of revolutionary socialism — the idea that the emancipation of the working class must be the act of the workers themselves. You cease to define your politics in terms of what you are for — working-class self-activity and democracy — and you frame it in terms of what you are against. So we see a lot of the left basing their politics on an "anti-imperialism" which is about making alliances or politically bigging up forces which are reactionary to the core. The common sense of the UK left is to support Hamas and Hezbollah, because they are "against Israel"; the Iranian regime because it is "against America"; and the Cuban regime because it is "against capitalism". Most recently, and tragically, we have started to see some leftists in the UK cheerlead for Islamists in the Muslim Brotherhood in Egypt, and the Ennahda Party in Tunisia. It doesn't matter that these forces are fundamentally hostile to the workers' movement and that whenever they have the chance they crack down on workers' self-organisation. You come to these dreadful political conclusions, cheerleading for fascist regimes, when you forget the central thing — working-class democracy and working-class self-emancipation.

Now, some people, including a broad tendency of thought that I think Laurie represents, have turned to alternative organisational models. As I say, I think that the urge to turn away from Stalinist forms of organising and find an atmosphere where activists can breathe more easily is correct. But I think that from the point of view of making a revolution, these strategies are simply not adequate.

Look at UK Uncut. It's a very impressive tool for organising one thing — protests outside of tax-dodging businesses. It provides a basic template, and periodic call-outs for action, which allow a lot of people to perform one kind of action very effectively. Taken on its own, this is good — it raises awareness of a given issue, knocks the authority of the rich, and gives people a good experience when they take part in these protests. But it can't go further than that. There is no overall programme for collectively debating the next step. There is no way of elaborating a body of ideas and taking ownership over them collectively.

You see already, in the frankly ludicrous actions bigging up John Lewis as an alternative model for the economy, how much difficulty the network has in elaborating an alternative vision for society. Followers of UKUncut on Twitter are basically reliant on the elite group at the centre of the network coming up with better ideas. That, or they have to think up ideas themselves, alone, and act on them, alone. This isn't out of malice from the organisers of UKUncut. The network just doesn't have the organisational structure to support an ongoing debate about a thoroughgoing alternative to capitalism. Likewise, in order to make a revolution, you will need to work for years to argue for socialist ideas and agitate in the workers' movement. This means doing a lot of different things — not just the same kind of thing over and over again. UK Uncut doesn't have the organisational structure to keep people in organised activity over a number of decades, nor does it have an organisational programme of collective education which could serve as a memory-bank of the movement. It is not adequate.

There is also a sensibility among the advocates of so-called "new", loosely-networked movements, that debate over ideas is unnecessarily harsh and that it disrupts unity — that the ideas will sort of sort themselves out over the course of the struggle. Likewise, there is the idea that ideological problems could be almost solved automatically by a loose milieu of campaign groups dissolving and reforming over and over again.

Now, this is true of UK Uncut — an ideologically loose movement can coalesce around one idea, without nitpicking about it, and pull off some great actions. But it's only one idea, not a full programme — and it's also a very easy sell. The idea that the banks should pay tax is a very easy sell. If you want to pull off actions around one basically uncontentious

29

idea that it's hard to disagree with, then you can make do with no ideological debate.

But if you want to convince people of the need for socialist revolution and for the workers to overthrow capitalism — you need to say things which are very unpopular, and figure out some ideas which are very complicated. You also need to draw conclusions from them. In order to do that, you can't say — "oh, the ideas will sort themselves out, let's just go leafleting". You need to think hard and collectively about these ideas, question them constantly to be sure they're right — and draw conclusions from them. A loose network where actions are disconnected from debates over ideas, and where debates are sort of relaxed and fluid because what everyone is going to do tomorrow does not really depend on them — that's fine if you're going with the flow. In fact, it is a recipe for following the path of least resistance. But if you want to think difficult and unpopular things, it's not adequate.

Some people in the movement are hostile to ideological debate, seeing it as a self-indulgence for privileged blokes, and a distraction from the struggle (sadly, they are sometimes right!). They think that we can make a movement that works without talking about ideas. Or, if they don't think that "officially", then in practice the way they operate as activists is informed by a disdain of political debate and political education.

Well, look at the workers of Tunisia. They have just overthrown one government, and they may be about to overthrow another. They're standing in the streets now, looking at each other and saying, "what next? we've got rid of one crappy system and we need to replace it with something else. But what?"

And who is going to answer that question? Who is going to say, "what next?" The Islamists? The Ba'athists? The new cabinet? At this point in the movement, the ideas that are dominant in the working class movement are going to determine everything. If you think that rigorous debate of ideas, and struggle for the right ideas, are not important in social movements, you are saying that you never expect the British working class to get to that point; you never expect us to be standing over a defeated government, asking "what next?". You don't think workers can make a revolution.

To finish: if you think that society is basically OK, or that it can be cleaned up with a tweak here, or a nudge there, then a variety of single issue campaigns, moving in loose convoy — tax avoidance here, tar sands there — that's sufficient.

But if you want to overthrow capitalism, then here-and-there tweaks and nudges will not do. You will need to say unpopular things, remember events you are not supposed to remember, face danger with comrades, and maybe alone. You will need to elaborate strategies for the mass movement, and work patiently to win people to them. In the twists and turns of a long and sometimes rapid class struggle, you will need to examine your ideas and those of your comrades to make sure you are on the right track. You — and not just you, but thousands of revolutionary class-fighters, need to learn, be trained, and train others, make sacrifices for an idea you constantly question, face enormous pressures, and make a long commitment. You can't do that alone. You need people around you who you can rely on, every day.

You can't use Twitter for that. It means a democratic party, a revolutionary organisation. And if I have convinced you of that, then join Workers' Liberty, and help us create one.

All feathered up: a new defence of anarchism

By Martin Thomas

Review of *Black Flame: The Revolutionary Class Politics of Anarchism and Syndicalism*, by Michael Schmidt and Lucien van der Walt (AK Press).

Originally serialised in *Solidarity* 203, 11 May 2011, 204, 18 May 2011, and 205, 25 May 2011

URL: bit.ly/l5GK0S

Variants of revolutionary syndicalism were major influences in the labour movements of several countries between the 1890s and World War One.

Their activists reckoned the work of the "political" socialists who spent much time on parliamentary electioneering to be deficient or even harmful, and focused effort on building up militant and democratic trade-union movements which they believed could be both the agency to overthrow capitalist power and the framework for future working-class administration of society. Some of them saw themselves as anarchists as well as syndicalists — "anarcho-syndicalists".

Schmidt and van der Walt, a journalist and an academic from Johannesburg, South Africa, tell us not only about the famous movements of France and Spain, Argentina and Mexico, but also about the less-known ones of China, Japan, and Korea.

Their book is not primarily a history. The authors reconstruct what the authors call a "broad anarchist tradition". They argued that it includes all of revolutionary syndicalism, not just the strands which called themselves anarchist. They present their own variant of "anarchism" as the most thorough and "sophisticated" development of the "tradition".

Their own version of anarchism is one in which the traditional points of dispute with Marxism are thinned down or, some of them, virtually given up; but it is accompanied by a horror of Marxism.

Schmidt and van der Walt never say straight out that they agree that a working-class overthrowing capitalism must organise from among itself a strong revolutionary authority to combat counter-revolution and consolidate the new order. They never directly disavow the traditional anarchist doctrine of the immediate abolition of any form of state.

But they pointedly do not repeat Bakunin's doctrine that the task of anarchists on the day after any revolution must be (through, so Bakunin held, a "secret" network of "invisible pilots") to thwart, divert, disrupt the victorious workers in their moves to coordinate their efforts democratically by electing a revolutionary authority.

JUNTA

They agree with "taking power in society" and "creating a coordinated system of governance".

They say "stateless governance", but the adjective "stateless", for them, seems to mean "radically democratic", "linked through delegates and mandates". In that sense, the Marxist-envisaged "workers' state" (or, in Lenin's term, "semi-state"), is "stateless".They accept the term "Revolutionary Junta" or "Workers' Republic" for the new authority. Although in one passage they claim that "class no longer exists" once the workers' revolution wins, in other passages they concede that counter-revolutionary groups will not disappear instantly, and accept the need for the new authority to organise "coordinated military defence" with "the best weaponry" (i.e. not just scattered militia groups with hand-weapons).

They agree that revolutionaries must build "a coherent... organisation, with a common analysis, strategy, and tactics, along with a measure of collective responsibility, expressed in a programme".

They use the term "party" sometimes and the term "vanguard" often for that. They agree that the party must be disciplined and tight. They quote with approval an account of the Nabat organisation led by Nestor Makhno: "The secretariat... was not merely 'technically' executive... It was also the movement's ideological 'pilot core'... controlling and deploying the movement's resources and militants".

While many anarchists today see the fact that Marxist organisations stretch themselves to produce and circulate weekly papers as infamous, Schmidt and van der Walt report on the extensive newspaper-producing and newspaper-selling culture of late 19th century anarchists with approval and pride.

They agree that the process of the working class preparing itself for revolution must include struggle for reforms. They approvingly quote Bakunin's statement, from the time (1867-8) when he was focused on trying to win over the bourgeois League for Peace and Freedom, that

33

"the most imperfect republic is a thousand times better than the most enlightened monarchy... The democratic regime lifts the masses up gradually to participation in public life". (Bakunin wrote different things later).

They emphasise that the value of the struggle for reforms lies in organisation from below in the struggle; but this is not a point of difference from Marxism. They explicitly dissent from the strands in anarchism which "refuse to deal with reforms, laws, and compromises".

Schmidt and van der Walt argue that revolutionary socialists should work systematically in trade unions, generally on building sustained and organised rank-and-file movements, and also sometimes contest elections for union office.

They agree that revolutionary socialists should take up battles for national liberation — "engage seriously with national liberation struggles and [aim] at supplanting nationalism, radicalising the struggle, and merging the national and class struggles in one revolutionary movement".

They oppose "identity politics" and the "cultural relativist" "claim made by some nationalists that certain rights are alien to their cultures and therefore unimportant or objectionable".

On all these points Schmidt and van der Walt have, in effect, a criticism of most of what calls itself anarchism today different only in shading from what we in Workers' Liberty would say. They are further away from conventional anarchism than is a group like the avowedly-Marxist Socialist Workers Party today, with its "One Solution, Revolution" slogan and its pretence that all "direct action" against the established order, even if it be led by Islamist clerical-fascists, is revolutionary and progressive.

Schmidt and van der Walt seem to stick to the old anarchist dogma of boycotting all electoral politics — "this would apply regardless of the mandates given... the wages paid to the parliamentarians, or the existence of other mechanisms to keep the parliamentarians accountable to their constituents" — and their account of anarchists in Korea who were elected to parliament there in the 1920s is disapproving. But they make little fuss about that issue.

In one passage they uphold the old anarchist idea of "the revolutionary general strike" as the only and more or less self-sufficient path to socialist revolution. But they make little of it, and other passages in the book imply a much less "fetishistic" view of the general strike.

ANTI-MARXISM

Their anti-Marxism is built not so much on a defence of traditional anarchist points as on a skewed presentation of Marxism.

For them, Marxism from its earliest days was proto-Stalinism. They construct their picture of Marxism by "reading back" from Stalinism.

They concede that "in claiming that his theory was scientific, Marx was no different from say, Kropotkin or Reclus, who saw their own theories as scientific". But somehow they also think that Marx's claim to have worked some things out and got some things right was more sinister than the similar claim made by anyone who ventures to trouble the public with their writings.

"Classical Marxism purported to alone understand the movement of history and express the fundamental interests of the proletariat... When [this] claim to a unique truth was welded to the strategy of the dictatorship of the proletariat... the formula for a one-party dictatorship through an authoritarian state was written".

Marxist theory was also, the authors claim, "teleological", seeing history as progressing mechanically "in a straight line towards a better future", through predetermined "stages". Marx (so they allege, on the basis of out-of-context snippets from his writings on India) "considered colonialism to be progressive". The "two-stage" doctrine developed for poorer countries by the Stalinists — that workers should first support the "national bourgeoisie" in "bourgeois-democratic revolution", and look to socialist revolution only at a later "stage" — was authentic Marxism, or so Schmidt and van der Walt claim.

They say that Marx had a relatively conservative view of socialist economic organisation: "Marx believed that the law of value would operate after the 'abolition of the capitalist mode of production'... the distribution of consumer goods under socialism would be organised through... markets". On that basis they claim the ideal of communist economics — supersession of the wages system; from each according to their ability, to each according to their need — as having been pioneered by the anarchist writer Peter Kropotkin.

The poor quality of Schmidt's and van der Walt's polemic on such points can be judged from their quotations. For example, they claim that Marx was cool on trade unions, and that it was the anarchists who explained and championed the potential of trade-union struggles.

"Marx complained that anarchists contended that workers 'must... organise themselves by trades unions' to 'supplant the existing states'..."

This is the passage from Marx (in a letter to Paul Lafargue of April

1870) from which Schmidt and van der Walt quote their snippets:

"Bakunin's programme [held that] the working class must not occupy itself with politics. They must only organise themselves by trades-unions. One fine day, by means of the International, they will supplant the place of all existing states. You see what a caricature he [Bakunin] has made of my doctrines!

"As the transformation of the existing States into Associations is our last end, we must allow the governments, those great Trade-Unions of the ruling classes, to do as they like, because to occupy ourselves with them is to acknowledge them. Why! In the same way the old socialists said: You must not occupy yourselves with the wages question, because you want to abolish wages labour, and to struggle with the capitalist about the rate of wages is to acknowledge the wages system!

"The ass has not even seen that every class movement, as a class movement, is necessarily and was always a political movement".

Marx was not hostile or cool about workers organising in trade unions. On the contrary: he was probably (in "The Poverty of Philosophy", his polemic against Proudhon in 1846, at a time when trade unions existed only in infant form) the first socialist to argue that trade-union organisation could be central in working-class emancipation.

Marx's objection was not to organising in trade unions, but to Bakunin's claim that the working class should not also "occupy itself with politics" (i.e. struggles for political reforms, and electoral activity).

Trotsky fought Stalinism to the death. But Schmidt and van der Walt claim he "envisaged socialism as 'authoritarian leadership... centralised distribution of the labour force... the workers' state... entitled to send any worker wherever his labour may be needed', with dissenters sent to labour camps if necessary".

The footnotes show that the words put in quote marks by Schmidt and van der Walt, as if they come from Trotsky, are culled not from Trotsky himself but from "pages 128, 132" of a book by one Wayne Thorpe.

Some of the words may have been taken by Thorpe from one of the polemics in which, in late 1920 — between the Bolsheviks' voting-down of Trotsky's first proposal in February 1920 of what would become the more liberal "New Economic Policy" and the adoption of the NEP itself, on Lenin's initiative, in early 1921 — Trotsky sought expedients to get the economy of revolutionary Russia into working order in the midst of civil war. None of the words was ever written by Trotsky as a statement of his vision of socialism. The quoted string of words was never written as a whole connected passage by Trotsky anywhere.

Schmidt and van der Walt claim further that: "The differences between [Stalinism and Trotskyism] should not be overstated: both embraced classical Marxism and its theories, both saw the USSR as post-capitalist and progressive, and both envisaged revolution by stages in less developed countries".

A footnote dismisses Trotsky's theory of permanent revolution as "no break with stage theory... simply a compression of the time frame".

Although Trotsky sketched the permanent revolution theory around 1905, before Stalin became prominent in politics and before Mao Zedong was politically active at all, they call permanent revolution an "echo" of "the two-stage formulation of Stalin and Mao". Why? Apparently because Trotsky recognised that issues such as land reform, national independence, and the replacement of autocracy by elected and constitutional government would be central in the first stages of mass mobilisation in capitalistically-undeveloped countries, and could not be "skipped over".

Marxism and Trotskyism are equated to Stalinism by Schmidt and van der Walt in order to clear the way for defence of "the broad anarchist tradition", with the authors' particular variants presented as the most thorough version of that tradition. The book raises, and offers a distinctive and unusual answer to, the question: what exactly is anarchism?

Its headline argument is that "the anarchist tradition" is in history the libertarian, class-struggle, "from-below" wing of the broad socialist current of thought. The authors have the same scheme of the history of socialism as the Marxist Hal Draper's famous pamphlet "The Two Souls of Socialism" — "socialism from below" versus "socialism from above" — but for them, unlike Draper, "the broad anarchist tradition" is socialism from below, and Marxism a chief species of socialism from above.

ANARCHISM = UNIONS?

Schmidt and van der Walt say that anarchism proper began only with the Bakunin wing of the First International, in the early 1870s. It was always a class-struggle movement.

Anarcho-syndicalism was not a fringe development from anarchism. On the contrary, "the most important strand in anarchism has always been syndicalism: the view that unions... are crucial levers of revolution, and can even serve as the nucleus of a free socialist order".

The "broad anarchist tradition" is thus for them, so to speak, what the "broad labour movement" is to Marxists.

We know that our views are for now in a small minority, and I think

37

Schmidt and van der Walt know that theirs are too. But we see ourselves as immersed in a broader movement which — despite all the follies and limitations which affect it now — is constantly pushed by its own activity, by its own logic and fundamentals, in our direction, for now in the shape of local flurries, and in future crises potentially wholesale.

For us, that broader movement is the labour movement; for Schmidt and van der Walt, it is the "broad anarchist tradition". Their definition allows them to deal with what they effectively admit to be the follies of much anarchism either by defining them out — for them, Max Stirner and Pierre-Joseph Proudhon were not anarchists at all — or by seeing them as vagaries and immaturities which, with good work, will be dispelled by the logic of the movement itself.

It allows them to claim as de facto anarchists many heroes who in life did not consider themselves anarchists at all. They claim the whole of the pre-1914 revolutionary syndicalist movement in France, and the whole of the IWW, for anarchism, though most of the leaders of the French movement and of the IWW did not see themselves as anarchists, and some, like Victor Griffuelhes, secretary of the French CGT in its heroic period, were explicitly political socialists.

They claim the avowed Marxists Daniel De Leon and James Connolly as "anarchists" because of their syndicalistic views, and seem (though this is not so explicit) also to claim the "council communists" Herman Görter, Anton Pannekoek, and Otto Rühle, and modern "autonomist Marxists", for their own.

Having "secured their flank" polemically by dismissing Marxism as proto-Stalinism (all but a few Marxists whom they claim as having really been anarchists), and by portraying many traditional anarchist dogmas as mere immature errors of the movement, they free themselves to maintain some traditional anarchist tenets at a more "theoretical" level.

Schmidt and van der Walt insist that anarchism is a class-struggle movement — indeed, *the* class-struggle movement. Their evidence for this, however, comes down to nothing more than the fact that most anarchists, like most activists for radical change generally and for obvious reasons, have seen the disadvantaged and dissatisfied as their constituency, and welcome strife.

They claim (wrongly, I think) that is libel to say that Bakunin looked to the "lumpenproletariat" ("underclass", paupers, people who live from begging, theft, dole, etc.) as the agency of revolution, rather than the core wage-working class. However, they are explicit in rejecting the Marxist views that the wage-working class — because of the way in which it is "trained, united, and organised by the very mechanism of the capitalist process of production" — is the unique and central agency of socialist revolution, and that the possibility of modern socialism depends on preconditions which are and can only be created by capitalism itself (the development of the human basis, the wage-working class, and of technology and communications).

For them, peasants are agents of socialist revolution just as much as wage-workers are, or more so. Schmidt and van der Walt quote Marx in polemic against Bakunin:

"He understands absolutely nothing about the social revolution, only its political phrases. Its economic conditions do not exist for him. As all hitherto existing economic forms, developed or undeveloped, involve the enslavement of the worker (whether in the form of wage-labourer, peasant etc.), he believes that a radical revolution is possible in all such forms alike.

"Still more! He wants the European social revolution, premised on the economic basis of capitalist production, to take place at the level of the Russian or Slavic agricultural and pastoral peoples, not to surpass this level... The will, and not the economic conditions, is the foundation of his social revolution".

And here they enter into dispute with the real Marx, not a proto-Stalinist "Marx" of their own invention.

"There [is] no need for the capitalist stage to be completed or even begun... It [is] not necessary to wait for capitalism to create the material basis for freedom; freedom would create its own material basis".

Although, as we've seen, Schmidt and van der Walt, unlike most anarchists, uphold the need for a disciplined revolutionary socialist party with a definite programme and a press, they are like traditional anarchists in that their conception of the "party" has little or no dimension of it being (in Trotsky's phrase) "the memory of the working class".

They disapprove of the Spanish anarchists joining the bourgeois governments of Catalonia and republican Spain during the Spanish civil war, but offer no discussion of lessons to be learned, or differentiations necessary in future anarchist movements if they are to avoid such things (which arose from the fact that the anarchists, having "rejected" all government, did not have a clear awareness of the difference between workers' government and bourgeois government, and so, when faced with the need for some coordinated authority for the war against the fascists, collapsed into joining bourgeois governments).

They claim the Mexican syndicalist movement for their "broad anar-

39

chist tradition", but comment on that movement's military alliance in 1915 with the bourgeois politicians Obregon and Carranza against revolutionary peasant armies only by labelling it "tragic".

The whole scheme of "socialism from below" versus "socialism from above" has the same deficiencies in the hands of Schmidt and van der Walt as it has in those of Hal Draper, despite the many merits of Draper's writings using the same scheme.

Unlike Marx's differentiation, in the Communist Manifesto, of socialist currents into working-class communism and various strands of what he called "reactionary socialism" influenced by other classes (feudal remnants, do-gooding bourgeoisie, petty bourgeoisie, etc.), this is an idealist scheme. On the one hand, the good, generous, democratic-minded guys and girls who want their socialism to be "from below"; on the other hand, the bad guys who wish it "from above".

Given that the world includes bad guys and girls as well as good ones, one wonders about the basis for hoping that the good ones will win out within the broad stream of socialist thought. History so far, after all, and socialist history as presented by Draper and by Schmidt and van der Walt, has been more like the old verse:

The rain it raineth every day
Upon the just and unjust fella,
But more upon the just because
The unjust hath the just's umbrella.

The sorting-out of socialists into good and bad types in this scheme tends to be arbitrary. Draper put all anarchists in the "from above" bag, on the basis of the real logic of Bakunin's wish for "invisible pilots" to thwart workers' attempts at organising their own democratic authority after revolution, and some real citations from Proudhon, but in a way that is unfair to many real-life anarchists. Schmidt and van der Walt, as we've seen, want to disavow Proudhon and Stirner as not anarchists at all, and claim De Leon and Connolly as good guys, as "from below" types.

Since revolution is not just a counterposition of "below" to "above", but an activity in which those "below" move to become "above", "from below" versus "from above" is not an adequate paraphrase of "by class struggle" versus "by petitioning or by bureaucratic or military coup".

Lenin put it like this: "Limitation, in principle, of revolutionary action to pressure from below and renunciation of pressure also from above is anarchism... He who does not understand the new tasks in the epoch of revolution, the tasks of action from above, he who is unable to determine the conditions and the programme for such action, has no idea whatever of the tasks of the proletariat in every democratic revolution".

MOVEMENT

Schmidt and van der Walt are right about one thing. Anarchism as a movement (or maybe the word "movement" is too definite, and the French word "mouvance", which has no exact English equivalent, would be better) does date from the 1872 split in the First International.

Bakunin and Kropotkin were much more its founders than Proudhon or Stirner. But what was that split really about? Was it — as it would have to be, if Schmidt and van der Walt's broad scheme were correct — a split between proto-Stalinism on one side, and class-struggle socialism on the other?

It was not. The issues, as stated by both sides, were:

One: political action by the working class. Bakunin's wing objected to the following resolution of the Hague Congress of the International, in September 1872:

"In its struggle against the collective power of the propertied classes, the working class cannot act as a class except by constituting itself into a political party, distinct from and opposed to all old parties formed by the propertied classes.

"This constitution of the working class into a political party is indispensable in order to insure the triumph of the social revolution, and of its ultimate end, the abolition of classes.

"The combination of forces which the working class has already effected by its economical struggles ought, at the same time, to serve as a lever for its struggles against the political power of landlords and capitalists.

"The lords of land and the lords of capital will always use their political privileges for the defence and perpetuation of their economical monopolies, and for the enslavement of labour. The conquest of political power has therefore become the great duty of the working class".

Two: the organisation of the International itself. Marx argued for an extension of the powers of the General Council (actually very modest: it amounted to no more than giving the General Council power to suspend units of the International, subject to a raft of safeguards). The Bakunin wing held that the future society must have no elected central authority, and the International must "prefigure" that future.

41

"The future society must be nothing else than the universalisation of the organisation that the International has formed for itself. We must therefore strive to make this organisation as close as possible to our ideal. How could one expect an egalitarian society to emerge out of an authoritarian organisation? It is impossible. The International, embryo of the future society, must from now on faithfully reflect our principles of federation and liberty, and must reject any principle tending toward authority and dictatorship". Marx remonstrated that this doctrine, despite all the "anti-authoritarians'" acclaim for grass-roots rebellion, meant trying to make the working-class struggle develop not according to its own logic but in subordination to "principles" deduced from the leaders' picture of an ideal future society.

"Had the Communards realised that the Commune was 'the embryo of the future human society', they would have thrown away all discipline and all weapons — things which must disappear as soon as there are no more wars..." "All arms with which to fight must be drawn from society as it is and the fatal conditions of this struggle have the misfortune of not being easily adapted to the idealistic fantasies which these doctors in social science have exalted as divinities, under the names of Freedom, Autonomy, Anarchy".

The "autonomous working men's sections" which the "anti-authoritarians" counterposed to an International led by the General Council would "become so many schools, with these gentlemen from the Alliance [Bakunin's friends] as their teachers. They formulate the idea through 'prolonged study'. They then 'bring it home to our working men's associations'. To them, the working class is so much raw material, a chaos which needs the breath of their Holy Spirit to give it form".

The 1872 split was not a clean sorting-out of "anti-authoritarians" even on Bakunin's definition. Many supported Bakunin, to one degree or another, who were not anarchists, but had grievances against a General Council which they saw as dominated by Marx — for example, George Eccarius, secretary of the International until May 1872; John Hales, his successor in that post; César de Paepe in Belgium; and the "Lassalleans" in Germany, whom Marx had criticised in 1868 for wanting "dictatorialism" and an excessively centralised regime in the workers' movement!

Another strand was complaint against the General Council and Marx for being too "German". Schmidt and van der Walt pick up that strand, stressed at the time by Bakunin. "Classical Marxists [saw] particular states as 'progressive'... Marx and Engels tended to cast Germany in the role of champion of progress in Europe... Their preference for Germany arguably hid an 'irrational nationalism'..."

They make much of Marx and Engels, in private correspondence at the start of the Franco-Prussian war in 1870, suggesting that their German comrades should vote for war credits (as the Lassalleans did) because this was for Germany a "war to defend its national existence" which it had been "forced into" by the aggression of the French emperor, Bonaparte. In fact the war had been deliberately engineered by the Prussian chancellor, Bismarck. Although Marx and Engels did not know that, they quickly came to endorse and acclaim the stance of Wilhelm Liebknecht and August Bebel in refusing war credits, and approvingly quoted a German workers' declaration:

"We declare the present war to be exclusively dynastic".

Marx and Engels were far from being German patriots. In the midst of the First International period, Marx wrote to Kugelmann: "Lassalle's successors oppose me... because they are aware of my avowed opposition to what the Germans call 'Realpolitik'. It is this sort of 'reality' which places Germany so far behind all civilised countries".

The real issue was what Schmidt and van der Walt tactfully call "an occasional tendency [by Bakunin] to stereotype the Germans", and the anarchist historian Max Nettlau called Bakunin's "nationalist psychosis". Whereas Marx, Engels, and their comrades quickly developed an independent working-class stance on the 1870 war, Bakunin explicitly sided with Imperial France. That difference did not become an issue in the split in the International, but Kropotkin's siding with France against Germany in World War One was a stance with real roots in anarchist tradition as well as a personal lapse.

In sum, the 1872 split was not between a Bakunin arguing for class-struggle socialism from below, and a Marx pressing towards Stalinism. The issues were those which Marxists since then have seen as central disputes with anarchism: whether workers should mobilise politically (in battles for political reform, and in independent working-class electoral activity), and whether workers should have a cohesive organisation based on the logic of class struggle within capitalism, or a loose network designed by reading back from a picture of an ideal future society.

A review of the background, in the trajectories of the First International and of Bakunin, confirms that assessment.

As Marx described it in his Inaugural Address for the First International, the defeat of the 1848 revolutions in Europe was followed by "an epoch of industrial fever, moral marasmus, and political reaction".

By the early 1860s, things were changing. The "industrial fever" had created sizeable industrial working classes in several countries, whereas in 1848 one had existed only in Britain.

The London Trades Council, though feeble by comparison with future trade-union organisations, became a force. The French workers gained some elbow-room. Oddly, in terms of the subsequent polemics, the major expression of this was an independent workers' candidature in March 1864 by Henri Tolain, who was a Proudhonist (proto-anarchist) and theoretically hostile to political action.

Solidarity with an uprising by the Polish people against Russian rule, in 1863, and with the North in the American Civil War (1861-5), further mobilised workers and the left.

The London Trades Council and Tolain's group organised a joint meeting in London in September 1864. The common account by biographers, and by Marx himself, is that Marx had withdrawn into his study and the British Library since the defeat of the 1848 movement. In fact he had remained involved in the affairs of the German worker-exiles in London (who were, given the repressive conditions in Germany, one of the nearest things there was a live German workers' movement). He was invited to the September 1864 meeting to represent the German workers.

He joined the General Council set up from the September 1864 meeting, bringing with him at least four veterans of his organisation from 1848, the Communist League.

In the earliest discussions, he was able to steer the new movement towards a class-struggle rather than just an abstract democratic political basis. He won acceptance for a "Preamble" to the Rules of the International which stated its aims in the following terms:

"The emancipation of the working classes must be conquered by the working classes themselves... the struggle for the emancipation of the working classes means not a struggle for class privileges and monopolies, but for equal rights and duties, and the abolition of all class rule;

"The economical subjection of the man of labour to the monopoliser of the means of labour — that is, the source of life — lies at the bottom of servitude in all its forms, of all social misery, mental degradation, and political dependence;

"The economical emancipation of the working classes is therefore the great end to which every political movement ought to be subordinate as a means;

"All efforts aiming at the great end hitherto failed from the want of solidarity between the manifold divisions of labour in each country, and from the absence of a fraternal bond of union between the working classes of different countries" — and therefore the International should organise that bond of solidarity.

The First International recruited substantially from its activity in supporting workers' strikes. It was initially a conglomerate of many shadings of socialist thought and many people who were not really socialists at all but rather radical democrats. In 1864 all the schools of socialist thought, Marx's too, lacked authoritative, readily-available texts codifying their ideas.

In 1864 nothing written by Marx was in general circulation. The Communist Manifesto of 1848 had had no new edition in any language since 1850. New editions in various languages appeared after 1865, as the International created a reading public for them, but only after.

Marx's "Contribution to a Critique of Political Economy" had been published in 1859; but only in German, and it was a severe economic text, with no immediate politics in it. Marx published "Capital" volume 1 in 1867 (in German), and a French translation came out in 1872-5 (an English translation, in 1886).

By patient argument within the International, Marx won a majority for three key ideas:

One: that strikes and trade unions must not only be supported, but were central to the working class organising and educating itself for emancipation. In a long debate in the General Council with an old Owenite socialist, John Weston, Marx refuted the alleged "iron law of wages" believed by many socialists at the time, according to which capitalism inevitably reduced wages to a subsistence minimum and all battles for higher wages must be fruitless.

Two: that the working class must aim for the expropriation of the capitalists and public ownership of the means of production. (The Proudhonists traditionally looked instead to the growth of a network of workers' cooperatives linked by "fair exchange" and crowding out capitalist production rather than expropriating the capitalists. Bakunin sided with Marx on this).

Three: that the working class must engage in political action (battles for reforms made by law, and electoral action) as well as economic struggle.

THE PARIS COMMUNE

The climax of Marx's activity in the First International was his writing of "The Civil War in France", the International's statement of solidarity with the Paris Commune of March-May 1871.

This was the major text by Marx likely to be read by the activists of the International.

"Marxism", for the purposes of the 1872 split, meant the ideas expressed in "The Civil War in France", and in the resolutions of the First International.

Engels, later, would summarise his and Marx's argument: "Of late, the Social-Democratic philistine has once more been filled with wholesome terror at the words: Dictatorship of the Proletariat. Well and good, gentlemen, do you want to know what this dictatorship looks like? Look at the Paris Commune. That was the dictatorship of the proletariat".

In the text itself Marx argued that the Commune was "essentially a working-class government... the political form at last discovered under which to work out the economic emancipation of labour".

It had shown that "the working class cannot simply lay hold of the ready-made state machinery, and wield it for its own purposes". The working class must create a new form of state, a semi-state as Lenin would call it.

The Commune had suppressed the standing army and substituted for it the armed people. It was made up of elected representatives who were accountable to their voters and easily recallable.

It was "a working, not a parliamentary, body, executive and legislative at the same time" — not like a bourgeois parliament, which, at best, limits and demands consultation from an executive government separate from it and standing above it.

It had done away with any separate, privileged bureaucratic corps of unelected state officials. "From the members of the Commune downwards, the public service had to be done at workmen's wages".

Explaining how his view differed from the anarchists, Marx wrote that "this new Commune, which breaks the modern State power, has been mistaken for a reproduction of the medieval Communes" (idealised by Bakunin, and, later, even more so by Kropotkin). "The Communal constitution has been mistaken for an attempt to break up into a federation of small states". (Bakunin and his friends insisted that the future society must be a federation of small local units). Local liberties should be guaranteed: but "the few but important functions which still would remain for a central government were not to be suppressed, as has been intentionally mis-stated, but were to be discharged by Communal... agents".

The "Civil War in France" was the main text on which Lenin would later draw to write his "State and Revolution", and the Bolsheviks to propose the rule of workers' councils (soviets) as the form of a workers' regime.

Although they are warm towards the "council communists", who favoured workers' councils but came to reject a centralised revolutionary party and electoral activity by revolutionary socialists — some of them also to reject trade-union activity — Schmidt and van der Walt make no explicit and definite comment on workers' councils, and in some passages seem to hold on to the pre-1914 revolutionary syndicalist line that trade unions, when smartened up enough, will embody workers' rule.

In any case, a split against a "Marxism" defined principally by "The Civil War in France" was assuredly not a split against a socialism of manipulating the existing state machine or "one-party dictatorship through an authoritarian state".

What did Bakunin and his friends say at the time? They supported the Commune and agreed with Marx on that against the English trade union leaders in the International who recoiled in horror from the Paris workers' revolution and Marx's fierce defence of it.

Like the Marxists, they would continue to honour the Commune and celebrate its anniversaries. As far as I know, they gave no direct reply to Marx's swipe at them in "The Civil War". Bakunin complained that "in order to fight the monarchist and clerical reaction they [the Commune] were compelled to organise themselves in a Jacobin manner, forgetting or sacrificing the first conditions of revolutionary socialism". Kropotkin, later, would be even more critical of the Commune as too "Jacobin".

Marx and Engels, by contrast, later, when the lapse of time had given licence for franker criticism of the Commune than would have been decent at the time of its bloody suppression by the French bourgeoisie, wrote (in effect) that the Commune had not been "Jacobin" enough — not forceful, radical, pushy enough. "In the economic sphere much was left undone which, according to our view today, the Commune ought to have done. The hardest thing to understand is certainly the holy awe with which they remain standing respectfully outside the gates of the Bank of France. This was also a serious political mistake. The bank in the hands of the Commune — this would have been worth more than ten thousand hostages [in terms of pressure on the bourgeois government at Versailles]".

47

In 1871 Bakunin wrote about his encounters with Marx in the 1840s. "As far as learning was concerned, Marx was, and is still, incomparably more advanced than I... He called me a sentimental idealist, and he was right; I called him vain, perfidious, and cunning..."

In 1872 the distinguishing mark of Bakunin and his friends was still "sentimental idealism" — the sentimental rejection of the necessary means of struggle in the name of a vague scheme for an instant ideal stateless future society.

Marx regarded the Bakunin wing as a relapse of a section of the International into the old utopian socialism.

"We cannot repudiate these patriarchs of socialism [the old utopian socialists], just as chemists cannot repudiate their forebears the alchemists, [but] we must at least avoid falling back into their mistakes, which, if we were to commit them, would be inexcusable".

Relapse was given momentum by the general backlash after the defeat of the Commune. In a similar way, the backlash after the defeat of the 1848 revolutions had led in September 1850 to a split in the Communist League in which the anti-Marx faction, according to Marx, fell into an approach where "the will, rather than the actual conditions, was stressed as the chief factor in the revolution" and "the word 'proletariat' [was] reduced to a mere phrase, like the word 'people' was by the democrats".

Later Plekhanov, in his pamphlet "Anarchism and Socialism", would expound Marx's thought in more detail, arguing that "in their criticism of the 'political constitution', the 'fathers' of anarchy always based themselves on the Utopian point of view", namely on the assertion that human nature favours liberty and solidarity, the state is an artificial imposition, and capitalism is the product of the state.

Bakunin, moving from his native Russia to study in Germany in 1840, became a revolutionary democrat in the 1840s. In 1849 he was praised by Marx for his role in a rising in Dresden.

Arrested after that rising, he spent eight years in jail, mostly in Russia and in atrocious conditions, and then four years in Siberian exile. In 1861 he escaped from Siberia to Western Europe.

Bakunin was still a revolutionary democrat rather than a strong socialist. At first his political plan was to work with the liberal exile Alexander Herzen. Then he flirted inconclusively with Garibaldi and with the Polish nationalist leader Mierosławski.

He came to call himself a "revolutionary socialist". In 1867-8 he and some friends entered and tried to take over the just-launched radical-bourgeois League for Peace and Freedom. He gave up within a year; but he wrote a elaborate document putting his views to the League — probably the longest and most complete political statement which Bakunin, notorious for rarely finishing things he started writing, ever published. It suggests that he then still saw his "revolutionary socialism" as more extreme than bourgeois democracy, rather than in irreducible class opposition to it.

He acclaimed the "complete emancipation... of industry and commerce... from the supervision and protection of the State"; remonstrated that "the majority of decent, industrious bourgeois" could quite well support his, Bakunin's, programme; limited his social-economic demands to changing "the law of inheritance, gradually at first, until it is entirely abolished as soon as possible"; and made no demand for the expropriation of capitalist property or the collective ownership of the means of production.

Disappointed in the League, he joined the International in 1868. His focus was still on anti-statism, and no doubt he still thought of Marx as "vain, perfidious, and cunning"; but his writings of that time suggest that he was genuinely won over by Marx's ideas as transmitted through the International.

They read as paraphrases — with a particular bias and twist, but paraphrases — of the general ideas of the International. He started work on a Russian translation of Marx's Capital, which he would never finish.

Diffuse and restless as ever in his thinking, in 1869-70 he got drawn into an alliance by a demented "nihilist", Sergei Nechayev, who held that the true revolutionary was defined by contempt for all moral standards, including in his dealings with his own comrades, and "must ally himself with the savage word of the violent criminal, the only true revolutionary in Russia"

He recoiled from Nechayev. Bakunin supported France in the 1870 Franco-Prussian war, and with a couple of comrades made an abortive attempt at an anarchist rising in Lyon (September 1870).

In 1870-2, finding sympathy for his resentments against Marx among Swiss activists of the International, Bakunin led a faction fight which ended in the split of September 1872. Soon after that, in October 1873, he resigned from his local organisation, the Jura Federation, on grounds of ill health and political disappointment. He spent most of the remaining time before his death in July 1876 in seclusion.

Some of Bakunin's ideas would be developed and codified, from the mid-1870s to World War One, by Peter Kropotkin, a much clearer and more systematic writer than Bakunin. But Bakunin's is not the record of a political figure who could in 1871-2 have represented a distinct "class-struggle" opposition to supposedly stodgier ideas coming from Marx.

The Bakunin wing's opposition in 1871-2 to electoral activity by socialists was not an exaggerated but understandable reaction against socialists allowing that activity to suck in too much of their energies and their hopes. At that time working-class electoral candidates were extremely rare.

Later new issues would arise. Socialists would allow electoral activity to suck in too much of their energies and their hopes.

The general principle established by Marx of the need for socialists to build and seek to broaden out trade unions would be complicated by the rise of trade-union bureaucracies, increasingly separating off into a distinct social layer mediating between workers and the bosses.

Those developments would give new life to anarchism, or at least to that wing of anarchism which swung away from the "propaganda of the deed" (assassinations of ruling-class figures) which had dominated anarchist activity in the 1880s to try to find a new basis in the growing workers' movements.

The revolutionary syndicalism of the decades before World War One was never (despite Schmidt and van der Walt) exclusively or even in majority anarchist; but some anarchists, such as Fernand Pelloutier and Emile Pouget in France, played a positive and important part in developing it.

It became, as Trotsky would put it, "a remarkable rough draft of revolutionary communism". Where the pre-1914 "political" socialists, too often, were content with the general perspective of building up and strengthening the workers' movement, the revolutionary syndicalists worked to transform, to invigorate, to democratise, to educate a workers' movement which they understood would tend to become conservatised and bureaucratised if left to its spontaneous course in capitalist society.

That dimension of socialist activity was taken up by the Communist International in its early years (1919-22), but quickly marginalised as the Communist International became Stalinised. Today groups like the Socialist Workers Party and the Socialist Party leave it marginalised, and in that sense the revolutionary syndicalism which Schmidt and van der Walt celebrate still has ideas to teach us, ideas which need to be rediscovered and redeveloped in today's conditions.

When the IWW leader Big Bill Haywood, in August 1920, read an appeal by the Communist International leadership written to try to convince IWW activists that the International was the best continuation of the IWW's tradition, he exclaimed: "Here is what we have been dreaming about; here is the IWW all feathered out!"

He was right, I think. Schmidt's and van der Walt's scheme, by contrast, is traditional anarchism all feathered up.

The AWL versus Anarchism

By Iain McKay (Editor, Anarchist FAQ)

Originally published to accompany a speech given at the Workers' Liberty event Ideas for Freedom, July 2011.

URL: anarchism.pageabode.com/anarcho/awl-versus-anarchism

According to the AWL's Martin Thomas, "Marxism is more 'bookish' than anarchism" and "insists more on the need for those who have decided to become consistent activists to study, to educate themselves."

Sadly, his account of anarchism published in *Solidarity* disproves it. This is easy to show, we need only compare his comments about anarchism to what anarchists like Michael Bakunin, Peter Kropotkin, Emma Goldman and a host of others argued.

Once you do, you discover the false nature of claims that Schmidt and van der Walt's "version of anarchism [in *Black Flame*] is one in which the traditional points of dispute with Marxism are thinned down or, some of them, virtually given up." Rather than being "further away from conventional anarchism" it simply repeats basic revolutionary anarchist ideas — as this leaflet proves. Is it not time for Marxists to stop producing strawman arguments against anarchism?

"The black flag is the flag of strikes" (Louise Michel)

"Schmidt and van der Walt say that anarchism... was always a class-struggle movement. Anarcho-syndicalism was not a fringe development from anarchism... [Their] version of anarchism is closer to Marxism than to traditional anarchism." (Martin Thomas (MT))

"Bakunin, Kropotkin, and Malatesta were not so naive as to believe that anarchism could be established over night. In imputing this notion to Bakunin, Marx and Engels wilfully distorted the Russian anarchist's views. Nor did the anarchists... believe that abolition of the state involved 'laying down of arms' immediately after the revolution, to use Marx's obscurantist choice of terms, thoughtlessly repeated by Lenin in *State and Revolution*. Indeed, much that passes for 'Marxism' in *State and Revolution* is pure anarchism — for example, the substitution of revolutionary militias for professional armed bodies and the substitution of organs of self-management for parliamentary bodies. What is authentically Marxist in Lenin's pamphlet is the demand for 'strict centralism,' the acceptance of a 'new' bureaucracy, and the identification of soviets with a state." (Murray Bookchin)

ANARCHISM AND THE CLASS STRUGGLE

"Some anarchists do [support class struggle]. Those are the anarcho-syndicalists, who on this issue have the same idea as Marxists do . . . But most schools of anarchism do not." (MT)

"between the proletariat and the bourgeoisie [is] an irreconcilable antagonism which results inevitably from their respective stations in life... the prosperity of the bourgeois class is incompatible with the prosperity and freedom of the workers... because... [it] is based on the exploitation and subjugation of the latter's labour... war between the proletariat and the bourgeoisie is unavoidable." (Michael Bakunin)

"When strikes spread out from one place to another, they come close to turning into a general strike. And with the ideas of emancipation that now hold sway over the proletariat, a general strike can result only in a great cataclysm which forces society to shed its old skin... strikes indicate a certain collective strength... each strike becomes the point of departure for the formation of new groups.

"The necessities of the struggle impel the workers to support one another... The more active the struggle becomes... the stronger and more extensive this federation of proletarians must become." (Bakunin)

"Anarchists have always advised taking an active part in those workers' organisations which carry on the *direct* struggle of Labour against Capital and its protector — the State." (Peter Kropotkin)

"It is this war of classes that we must concentrate upon... Those who appreciate the urgent need of co-operating in great struggles... must organise the preparedness of the masses for the overthrow of both capitalism and the state. Industrial and economic preparedness is what the workers need. That alone leads to revolution at the bottom... That alone will give the people the means to take their children out of the slums, out of the sweat shops and the cotton mills... That alone leads to economic and social freedom." (Emma Goldman)

"strikes and trade unions must not only be supported, but were central to the working class organising and educating itself for emancipation." (MT)

"the strike... is the beginnings of the social war of the proletariat against the bourgeoisie... Strikes are a valuable instrument from two points of view. Firstly, they electrify the masses... awaken in them the feeling of the deep antagonism which exists between their interests and those of the bourgeoisie... secondly they help immensely to provoke and establish between the workers of all trades, localities and countries the consciousness and very fact of solidarity: a twofold action, both negative and positive, which tends to constitute directly the new world of the proletariat, opposing it almost in an absolute way to the bourgeois world." (Bakunin)

"Since the enemy on whom we declare war is capital, it is against capital that we have to direct our efforts... the great struggle... is an essentially *economic* struggle To be able to make the revolution, the mass of workers will have to organise themselves. Resistance and the strike are excellent means of organisation for doing this... It is a question of organising societies of resistance for all trades in each town... of federating them... Workers' solidarity must... be practised each day between all trades and all nations." (Kropotkin)

"the *direct* struggle of Labour against Capital... and the State... permits the worker to obtain some temporary improvements in the present conditions of work, while it opens his eyes to the evil done by Capitalism and the State that supports it, and wakes up his thoughts concerning the possibility of organising consumption, production, and exchange without the intervention of the capitalist and the State." (Kropotkin)

"Anarchism... stands for direct action... Trade unionism, the economic area of the modern gladiator, owes its existence to direct action... In France, in Spain, in Italy, in Russian, nay even in England... direct, revolutionary economic action has become so strong a force in the battle for industrial liberty as to make the world realise the tremendous importance of labour's power. The General Strike [is] the supreme expression of the economic consciousness of the workers... Today every great strike, in order to win, must realise the importance of the solidaric general protest." (Goldman)

"the most powerful force for social transformation is the working class movement... Through the organisations established for the defence of their interests, workers acquire an awareness of the oppression under which they live and of the antagonisms which divide them from their employers, and so begin to aspire to a better life, get used to collective struggle and to solidarity." (Errico Malatesta)

"only the right organisation of the workers can accomplish what we are

striving for... Organisation from the bottom up, beginning with the shop and factory, on the foundation of the joint interests of the workers everywhere... alone can solve the labour question and serve the true emancipation of man." (Alexander Berkman)

"Trade-union struggle.... yields the biggest, most stable, and most powerful organisations, and best enables the socialists to develop dialogue with and gain organised influence among their fellow-workers." (MT)

"the International has been... the work of the proletariat itself . . . It was their keen and profound instinct as workers... which impelled them to find the principle and true purpose of the International. They took the common needs already in existence as the foundation and saw the *international organisation of economic conflict against capitalism* as the true objective of this association. In giving it exclusively this base and aim, the workers at once established the entire power of the International. They opened wide the gates to all the millions of the oppressed and exploited.... organising local, national and international strikes... establishing national and international trade unions." (Bakunin)

"what is the natural organisation of the masses? It is one based on the different occupations of their actual daily life, on their various kinds of work, organisations according to their occupations, trade organisations. When all industries, including the various branches of agriculture, are represented in the International, its organisation, the organisation of the masses of the people, will be finished." (Bakunin)

"only the trade union sections can give their members... practical education and consequently only they can draw into the organisation of the International the masses of the proletariat, those masses without whose practical co-operation... the Social Revolution will never be able to triumph." (Bakunin)

"Revolutionary Anarchist Communist propaganda within the Labour Unions had always been a favourite mode of action in the Federalist or 'Bakuninist' section of the International Working Men's Association. In Spain and in Italy it had been especially successful. Now it was resorted to, with evident success, in France and *Freedom* eagerly advocated this sort of propaganda." (Kropotkin)

"But what anarchists — again with the exception of anarcho-syndicalists — lack is a coherent idea of how the minority can act today so as best to contribute to majority action tomorrow." (MT)

"the workers' world... is left with but a single path, that of *emancipation through practical action...* It means workers' solidarity in their struggle against the bosses. It means *trades-unions, organisation, and the federation of resistance funds...* reducing working hours and increasing salary... the International... will propagandise its principles... organise across the frontiers of all countries... so that when the revolution ... breaks out... the International will be a real force ... [an] international organisation of workers' associations... capable of replacing this... world of States and bourgeoisie." (Bakunin)

"only the trade union sections can give their members... practical education and consequently only they can draw into the organisation of the International the masses of the proletariat, those masses without whose practical co-operation... the Social Revolution will never be able to triumph." (Bakunin)

"Revolutionary Anarchist Communist propaganda within the Labour Unions had always been a favourite mode of action in the Federalist or 'Bakuninist' section of the International Working Men's Association. In Spain and in Italy it had been especially successful. Now it was resorted to, with evident success, in France and *Freedom* eagerly advocated this sort of propaganda." (Kropotkin)

"But what anarchists — again with the exception of anarcho-syndicalists — lack is a coherent idea of how the minority can act today so as best to contribute to majority action tomorrow." (MT)

"the workers' world... is left with but a single path, that of *emancipation through practical action...* It means workers' solidarity in their struggle against the bosses. It means *trades-unions, organisation, and the federation of resistance funds...* reducing working hours and increasing salary... the International... will propagandise its principles... organise across the frontiers of all countries... so that when the revolution ... breaks out... the International will be a real force ... [an] international organisation of workers' associations... capable of replacing this... world of States and bourgeoisie." (Bakunin)

"Faithful to the anarchist traditions of the International... [Spanish anarchists] remain in the working class, they struggle with it... They bring their energy to the workers' organisation and work to build up a force which will crush Capital on the day of the revolution: the revolutionary trade association. Trade sections, federations of all the trades....

"We could not do less than advise the French workers to take up again ... the traditions of the International, to organise themselves outside all political parties by inscribing on their banner *solidarity in the struggle against Capital."* (Kropotkin)

"Bakunin did not see the working class as the central agent of revolution. He considered peasants and the urban unemployed, beggars, petty criminals, etc. to be much more potent revolutionary forces." (MT)

"it is necessary to organise the power of the proletariat. But this organisation must be the work of the proletariat itself... Organise, constantly organize the international militant solidarity of the workers, in every trade and country, and remember that however weak you are as isolated individuals or districts, you will constitute a tremendous, invincible power by means of universal co-operation." (Bakunin)

"for the International to be a real power, it must organise within its ranks the immense majority of the proletariat... The workers... join the International for... solidarity in the struggle for full economic rights against the oppressive exploitation by the bourgeoisie ... the *organisation of solidarity in the economic struggle of labour against capitalism."* (Bakunin)

"to create a people's force capable of crushing the military and civil force of the State, it is necessary to organise the proletariat." (Bakunin)

"a living, powerful, socialist movement... can be made a reality only by the awakened revolutionary consciousness, the collective will, and the organization of the working masses themselves." (Bakunin)

"a new social order based... upon the collective appropriation of the instruments of labour... [created] by the development and organisation... of the social (and, by consequence, anti-political) power of the working masses." (Bakunin)

"The general principle established by Marx of the need for socialists to build and seek to broaden out trade unions would be complicated by the rise of trade-union bureaucracies, increasingly separating off into a distinct social layer mediating between workers and the bosses." (MT)

"Having convinced themselves that what they would like their [union] sections to do is what the membership actually wants, the committees make decisions for them without even bothering to consult them... The construction workers' section simply left all decision-making to their committees... This is very good for the committees, but not at all favourable for the social, intellectual, and moral progress of the collective power of the International. In this manner power gravitated to the committees... the sections could defend their rights and their autonomy in only one way: the workers called general membership meetings. Nothing arouses the antipathy of the committees more than these popular [union] assemblies... the items on the agenda were amply discussed and the most progressive opinion prevailed... In these assemblies... great numbers of previously passive workers, caught up in the general camaraderie, repudiated their leaders and voted against their resolutions." (Bakunin)

ANARCHISM AND ANARCHO-SYNDICALISM

"anarcho-syndicalism ... is the version of anarchism that identifies the society of the future as a federation of industries each run by the trade-union of the workers in the industry." (MT)

"Bakunin's programme... [is that] the working class must not occupy itself with politics. They must only organise themselves by trades-unions... [and] by means of the International, they will supplant the place of all existing states." (Marx)

"The future social organisation must be made solely from the bottom up, by the free association or federation of workers, firstly in their unions, then in the communes, regions, nations and finally in a great federation, international and universal." (Bakunin)

"The organisation of the trade sections and... the Chambers of Labour... bear in themselves the living seeds of the new society which is to replace the old world. They are creating not only the ideas, but also the facts of the future itself." (Bakunin)

"we hold that the granges, trade-unions, Knights of Labour assemblies, etc., are the embryonic groups of the ideal anarchistic society." (Lucy Parsons)

"Unions... are natural organs for the direct struggle with capitalism and for the composition of the future social order." (Kropotkin)

"In times when working-class organisation and struggle have run at a high level, many anarchists have gone over to anarcho-syndicalism, i.e. to much the same idea as Marxists about the centrality of the wage-working class and its everyday struggles."(MT)

"Bakunin has a peculiar theory... carry on propaganda, heap abuse on the state, organise, and when all the workers... are own over, depose all the authorities, abolish the state and replace it with the organisation of the International." (Engels)

"I have... never ceased to urge the comrades into that direction which the syndicalists, forgetting the past, call *new*, even though it was already glimpsed and followed, in the International, by the first of the anarchists." (Malatesta)

"anarchists... do not seek to constitute, and invite the working men not to constitute, political parties in the parliaments. Accordingly, since the foundation of the International Working Men's Association in 1864-1866, they have endeavoured to promote their ideas directly amongst the labour organisations and to induce those unions to a direct struggle against capital, without placing their faith in parliamentary legislation." (Kropotkin)

"the split in the revolutionary movement... one, under Marx and Engels, aiming at political conquest; the other, under Bakunin and the Latin workers, forging ahead along industrial and Syndicalist lines... Syndicalism is, in essence, the economic expression of Anarchism." (Goldman)

"Modern Anarcho-Syndicalism is a direct continuation of those social aspirations which took shape in the bosom of the First International and which were best understood and most strongly held by the libertarian wing of the great workers' alliance." (Rudolf Rocker)

"Unlike other variants of anarchism, anarchosyndicalism focuses on the wage-working class. It has a coherent idea of what to do in un-revolutionary times: build up the unions which will later be the instruments of revolution." (MT)

"Organise the city proletariat in the name of revolutionary Socialism, and in doing this, unite it into one preparatory organisation together with the peasantry." (Bakunin)

"The union is absolutely necessary. It is the only form of workers' grouping which permits the direct struggle to be maintained against capital without falling into parliamentarism." (Kropotkin)

"With an admirable tenacity they [the anarchist workers] organise their unions, within each nation and internationally, and with a still more admirable ardour they prepare the great coming struggle of Labour against Capital: the coming of the international general strike." (Kropotkin)

"direct action and the direct struggle of the workers against capital.... workers are realising that they alone must free themselves... making use of Direct Action as the preparatory means for the final battle of exploited Labour against... Capital." (Kropotkin)

"the strength of the worker... is in the shop and factory, in the mill and mine. It is there that he must organise; there, on the job... Every shop and factory should have its special committee... Its members are recalled at will and others selected in their place... It is the workers who decide the matters at issue and carry their decisions out through the shop committees... [This is] the form of organisation that labour needs... These shop and factory committees, combined with similar bodies in other mills and mines, associated locally, regionally, and nationally, would constitute a new type of labour organisation." (Berkman)

"The Bakunin wing's opposition.... to electoral activity by socialists was not an exaggerated but understandable reaction against socialists allowing that activity to suck in too much of their energies and their hopes.... Socialists would allow electoral activity to suck in too much of their energies and their hopes... socialists who in their majority turned out to be unprincipled parliamentary reformists."(MT)

"The worker-deputies, transplanted into a bourgeois environment, into an atmosphere of purely bourgeois ideas, will in fact cease to be workers and, becoming Statesmen, they will become bourgeois... For men do not make their situations; on the contrary, men are made by them." (Bakunin)

"Hardly any of these ideas are new: almost all are derived from the Bakuninist section of the old International." (Bertrand Russell)

ANARCHISM AND THE MEDIEVAL COMMUNE

"Medieval Communes... [were] idealised by Bakunin, and, later, even more so by Kropotkin." (MT)

"Mazzini, in his hatred of the Paris Commune, has gone to the extreme of sheer foolishness. He maintains that the... revolution in Paris would lead us back to the medieval ages... He does not understand, poor fellow, that between the commune of the Middle Ages and the modern commune there is the vast difference which the history of the last five centuries wrought." (Bakunin)

"Between the Commune of the middle ages and that...established today... there will be plenty of essential differences: a veritable abyss opened up by six or seven centuries of human development... all the great cities will unfurl the same flag." (Kropotkin)

ANARCHISM AND CAPITALISM

"Bakunin.... made no demand for the expropriation of capitalist property or the collective ownership of the means of production." (MT)

"organise society in such a manner that every individual ... should find... equal means for the development of his or her diverse faculties and their utilisation in his or her work... rendering impossible the exploitation of anyone's labour... enable every individual to enjoy the social wealth... only in so far as he contributes directly toward the creation of that wealth... the serious realisation of liberty, justice, and peace will be impossible so long as the majority of the population... is condemned to... producing all the wealth.... and receiving in return only such a small part thereof ... [Hence] the necessity of a radical social and economic reconstruction, having for its aim the emancipation of people's labour from the yoke of capital and property owners." (Bakunin)

"the land, the instruments of work and all other capital... become the collective property of the whole of society and be utilised only by the workers, in other words by the agricultural and industrial associations." (Bakunin)

"Proudhon... did not even see industrial capital as exploitative." (MT)

"property... degrades us, by making us servants and tyrants to one another.... wage-worker[s]... work under a master ... the surplus of labour, essentially collective, passes entirely, like the revenue, to the proprietor... the worker, whose share of the collective product is constantly confiscated by the entrepreneur, is always on his uppers, while the capitalist is always in profit." (Proudhon)

"the [Anarchist] assertion that... capitalism is the product of the state." (MT)

"The State is authority, domination, and force, organised by the property-owning and so-called enlightened classes against the masses... the State's domination... [is] that of the privileged classes who it solely represents." (Bakunin)

"The State is there to protect exploitation, speculation and private property." (Kropotkin)

"the State... and Capitalism are facts and conceptions which we cannot separate from each other. In the course of history these institutions have developed, supporting and reinforcing each other." (Kropotkin)

"the State is necessary *only* to maintain or protect property and monopoly. It has proven efficient in that function only." (Goldman)

"[Bakunin's] repeated declaration that the first step in any revolution should be to have 'all legal papers consigned to the flames', and all public regulation of debts and taxes abolished, was designed to appeal to the peasant for whom 'the state' is nothing but the unwelcome tax-collector." (MT)

"the revolution must set out from the first to radically and totally destroy the State... The natural and necessary consequence of this destruction will be... dissolution of army, magistracy, bureaucracy, police and priesthood.... confiscation of all productive capital and means of production on behalf of workers' associations, who are to put them to use." (Bakunin)

"Paris will naturally make haste to organise itself as best it can, in revolutionary style, after the workers have joined into associations and made a clean sweep of all the instruments of labour, every kind of capital and building; armed and organised by streets and *quartiers*, they will form the revolutionary federation of all the *quartiers*, the federative commune... All the French and foreign revolutionary communes will then send representatives to organise the necessary common services... and to organise common defence against the enemies of the Revolution, together with propaganda, the weapon of revolution, and practical revolutionary solidarity with friends in all countries against enemies in all countries." (Bakunin)

"in order that the peasants rise up, it is absolutely necessary that the initiative in this revolutionary movement be taken up by the city workers... who combine in themselves the instincts, ideas, and conscious will of the Social Revolution." (Bakunin)

"the working class must aim for the expropriation of the capitalists and public ownership of the means of production." (MT)

"under universal association, ownership of the land and of the instruments of labour is *social* ownership . . . We want the mines, canals, railways handed over to democratically organised workers' associations... We want these associations to be models for agriculture, industry and trade, the pioneering core of that vast federation of companies and societies woven into the common cloth of the democratic and social Republic." (Proudhon)

"all the capital, the factories, and all instruments of work and raw materials to go to the associations, and the land to those who cultivate it with their own hands." (Bakunin) "the serious, final, complete liberation of the workers is possible only upon one condition: that of the appropriation of capital, that is, of raw material and all the tools of labour, including land, by the whole body of the workers." (Bakunin)

"a successful uprising... [involves] the complete political, juridical, financial, and administrative liquidation of the State, and of political and privately owned or controlled (but not strictly) personal property; the demolition of all the functions, services, and powers of the State... workers' associations would then take possession of all the tools of production as well as all buildings and capital." (Bakunin)

"The next revolution must from its inception bring about the seizure of the entire social wealth by the workers in order to transform it into common property. This revolution can succeed only through the workers, only if the urban and rural workers everywhere carry out this objective themselves. To that end, they must initiate their own action in the period *before the revolution*; this can happen only if there is a strong *workers' organisation*." (Kropotkin)

"Expropriation — that is the guiding word of the coming revolution, without which it will fail in its historic mission: the complete expropriation of all those who have the means of exploiting human beings; the return to the community of the nation of everything that in the hands of anyone can be used to exploit others." (Kropotkin)

"To destroy radically this oppression... all people must be convinced of their right to the means of production, and be prepared to exercise this basic right by expropriating the landowners, the industrialists and financiers, and putting all social wealth at the disposal of the people." (Malatesta)

ANARCHISM AND DEFENCE OF THE REVOLUTION

"*[Black Flame] concede[s] that counter-revolutionary groups will not disappear instantly, and accept the need for... 'coordinated military defence' with 'the best weaponry' (i.e. not just scattered militia groups...).*" (MT)

"In order to defend the revolution... volunteers will... form a communal militia. But no commune can defend itself in isolation. So it will be necessary to radiate revolution outward, to raise all of its neighbouring communes in revolt... and to federate with them for common defence." (Bakunin)

"the peasants, like the industrial city workers, should unite by federating the fighting battalions, district by district, assuring a common co-ordinated defence against internal and external enemies." (Bakunin)

"creation of voluntary militia, without powers to interfere as militia in the life of the community, but only to deal with any armed attacks by the forces of reaction to re-establish themselves, or to resist outside intervention." (Malatesta)

"your duty, as an Anarchist, [is] to protect your liberty, to resist coercion and compulsion.... The armed workers and peasants are the only effective defence of the revolution. By means of their unions and syndicates they must always be on guard against counter-revolutionary attack." (Berkman)

ANARCHISM AND THE PARIS COMMUNE

"The Commune.... was made up of elected representatives who were accountable to their voters and easily recallable... 'a working, not a parliamentary, body, executive and legislative at the same time'... not like a bourgeois parliament.... [with] an executive government separate from it and standing above it." (MT)

"the imperative mandate, and permanent revocability are the most immediate and incontestable consequences of the electoral principle. It is the inevitable program of all democracy." (Proudhon)

"It is up to the National Assembly, through organisation of its committees, to exercise executive power, just the way it exercises legislative power... Besides universal suffrage and as a consequence of universal suffrage, we want implementation of the imperative mandate. Politicians balk at it! Which means that in their eyes, the people, in electing representatives, do not appoint mandatories but rather abjure their sovereignty!" (Proudhon)

"the collective ownership of property by freely organised producers' associations, and... federation of communes, to replace the... State... Proudhonism, greatly developed and taken to its ultimate conclusion by the proletariat of the Latin countries.... has just attempted its first striking and practical demonstration in the Paris Commune." (Bakunin)

"The climax of Marx's activity in the First International was his writing of 'The Civil War in France', the International's statement of solidarity with the Paris Commune of March-May 1871. This was the major text by Marx likely to be read by the activists of the International." (MT)

"The general effect [of the Commune] was so striking that the Marxists themselves, who saw their ideas upset by the uprising, found themselves compelled to take their hats off to it. They went further, and proclaimed that its programme and purpose were their own, in face of the simplest logic... This was a truly farcical change of costume." (Bakunin)

ANARCHISM AND WORKERS' COUNCILS

"Workers then need much broader and more flexible organisations than even the trade unions... workers' councils." (MT)

"Toilers count no longer on anyone but yourselves. Do not demoralise and paralyse your growing strength by being duped into alliances with bourgeois Radicalism... organise outside of it the forces of the proletariat. The bases of this organisation are already completely given: they are the workshops and the federation of workshops.... instruments of struggle against the bourgeoisie, and their federation, not only national, but international." (Bakunin)

"the federative Alliance of all working men's associations... constitute the Commune... [the] Communal Council [is] composed of... delegates... vested with plenary but accountable and removable mandates... constitute the federation of insurgent associations, communes and provinces.... organise a revolutionary force capable defeating reaction... [and for] self-defence... [The] revolution everywhere must be created by the people, and supreme control must always belong to the people organised into a free federation of agricultural and industrial associations... organised from the bottom upwards by means of revolutionary delegation." (Bakunin)

"there is no other system but that of the republic as a commune, the republic as a federation, a Socialist and a genuine people's republic — the system of Anarchism... a free federation from below upward, of workers associations, industrial as well as agricultural... first into a commune, then a federation communes into regions, of regions into nations, and of nations into international fraternal association." (Bakunin)

"workers' organisations... must take the place of existing capitalist exploitation and the state...it is the duty and the task of the workers' organisations to work out the new form of society." (Kropotkin)

"The Paris Commune... had shown that 'the working class cannot simply lay hold of the ready-made state machinery, and wield it for its own purposes'. The working class must create a new form of state, a semi-state as Lenin would call it . . . a split against a 'Marxism' defined principally by 'The Civil War in France' was assuredly not a split against a socialism of manipulating the existing state machine." (MT)

"[This quote from *The Civil War in France*] is simply a question of showing that the victorious proletariat must first refashion the old bureaucratic, administrative centralised state power before it can use it for its own purposes." (Engels)

"the way to show political power [in Britain] lies open to the working class. Insurrection would be madness where peaceful agitation would more swiftly and surely do the work." (Marx)

"the institutions, customs and traditions in the different countries must be taken into account; and we do not deny the existence of countries like America, England, and if I knew your institutions better I might add Holland, where the workers may achieve their aims by peaceful means." (Marx)

"[In Holland] only a few changes will have to be made to establish that free self-government by the working class." (Engels)

"the only organisation the victorious working class finds ready-made for use, is that of the State. It may require adaptation to the new functions. But to destroy that at such a moment, would be to destroy the only organism by means of which the working class can exert its newly conquered power." (Engels)

"the republic... is the *ready-for-use* form for the future rule of the proletariat." (Engels)

"If one thing is certain it is that our Party and the working class can only come to power under the form of a democratic republic. This is even the specific form for the dictatorship of the proletariat." (Engels)

"The 'Civil War in France' was the main text on which Lenin would later draw to write his 'State and Revolution', and the Bolsheviks to propose the rule of workers' councils (soviets) as the form of a workers' regime." (MT)

"the dictatorship of the proletariat cannot be exercised through an organisation embracing the whole of the class, because in all capitalist countries (and not only over here, in one of the most backward) the proletariat is still so divided, so degraded, and so corrupted in parts... that an organisation taking in the whole proletariat cannot directly exercise proletarian dictatorship. It can be exercised only by a vanguard... Such is the basic mechanism of the dictatorship of the proletariat, and the essentials of transition from capitalism to communism... for the dictatorship of the proletariat cannot be exercised by a mass proletarian organisation." (Lenin)

"The revolutionary dictatorship of a proletarian party is for me not a thing that one can freely accept or reject: It is an objective necessity imposed upon us by the social realities — the class struggle, the heterogeneity of the revolutionary class, the necessity for a selected vanguard in order to assure the victory. The dictatorship of a party belongs to the barbarian prehistory as does the state itself, but we can not jump over this chapter... The revolutionary party (vanguard) which renounces its own dictatorship surrenders the masses to the counter-revolution... Abstractly speaking, it would be very well if the party dictatorship could be replaced by the 'dictatorship' of the whole toiling people without any party, but this presupposes such a high level of political development among the masses that it can never be achieved under capitalist conditions." (Trotsky)

"Trotsky fought Stalinism to the death." (MT)

"This growing replacement of the party by its own apparatus is promoted by a 'theory' of Stalin's which denies the Leninist principle, inviolable for every Bolshevik, that the dictatorship of the proletariat is and can be realized only through the dictatorship of the party... The dictatorship of the proletariat imperiously demands a single and united proletarian party." (Trotsky)

"The Workers' Opposition has come out with dangerous slogans, making a fetish of democratic principles! They place the workers' right to elect representatives above the Party, as if the party were not entitled to assert its dictatorship even if that dictatorship temporarily clashed with the passing moods of the workers' democracy. It is necessary to create amongst us the awareness of the revolutionary birthright of the party, which is obliged to maintain its dictatorship, regardless of temporary wavering even in the working classes. This awareness is for us the indispensable element. The dictatorship does not base itself at every given moment on the formal principle of a workers' democracy." (Trotsky)

"The very same masses are at different times inspired by different moods and objectives. It is just for this reason that a centralised organisation of the vanguard is indispensable. Only a party, wielding the authority it has won, is capable of overcoming the vacillation of the masses themselves... if the dictatorship of the proletariat means anything at all, then it means that the vanguard of the proletariat is armed with the resources of the state in order to repel dangers, including those emanating from the backward layers of the proletariat itself." (Trotsky)

"Schmidt and van der Walt claim [Trotsky] 'envisaged socialism as 'authoritarian leadership... centralised distribution of the labour force... the workers' state... entitled to send any worker wherever his labour may be needed', with dissenters sent to labour camps if necessary'... None of the words was ever written by Trotsky as a statement of his vision of socialism." (MT)

Trotsky's *Terrorism and Communism* (1920):

"the only solution to economic difficulties from the point of view of both principle and of practice is to treat the population of the whole country as the reservoir of the necessary labour power... and to introduce strict order into the work of its registration, mobilisation and utilisation."

"We have... been accused of having substituted for the dictatorship of the Soviets the dictatorship of our party. Yet... the dictatorship of the Soviets became possible only by means of the dictatorship of the party.... In this 'substitution' of the power of the party for the power of the working class there is nothing accidental, and in reality there is no substitution at all."

"we can have no way to Socialism except by the authoritative regulation of the economic forces and resources of the country, and the centralised distribution of labour-power in harmony with the general State plan."

"I consider if the civil war had not plundered our economic organs of all that was strongest, most independent, most endowed with initiative, we should undoubtedly have entered the path of one-man management in the sphere of economic administration much sooner and much less painfully."

"the road to Socialism lies through a period of the highest possible intensification of the principle of the State... Just as a lamp, before going out, shoots up in a brilliant flame, so the State, before disappearing, assumes the form of the dictatorship of the proletariat, i.e., the most ruthless form of State, which embraces the life of the citizens authoritatively in every direction... No organisation except the army has ever controlled man with such severe compulsion as does the State organisation of the working class in the most difficult period of transition. It is just for this reason that we speak of the militarisation of labour."

"When the IWW leader Big Bill Haywood, in August 1920, read an appeal by the Communist International leadership written to try to convince IWW activists that the International was the best continuation of the IWW's tradition, he exclaimed: 'Here is what we have been dreaming about; here is the IWW all feathered out!'" (MT)

"The Russian Soviet Republic... is the most highly centralised government that exists. It is also the most democratic government in history. For all the organs of government are in constant touch with the working masses, and constantly sensitive to their will." (Zinoviev to the IWW)

"soviet rule in Russia could not have been maintained for three years — not even three weeks — without the iron dictatorship of the Communist Party... the dictatorship of the working class can be achieved only by the dictatorship of its vanguard, i.e., by the Communist Party... All questions... on which the fate of the proletarian revolution depends... are decided... mostly in the framework of the party organisations... Control by the party over soviet organs, over the trade unions." (Zinoviev, 1920)

"Today, people like Kautsky come along and say that in Russia you do not have the dictatorship of the working class but the dictatorship of the party. They think this is a reproach against us. Not in the least! We have a dictatorship of the working class and that is precisely why we also have a dictatorship of the Communist Party. The dictatorship of the Communist Party is only a function, an attribute, an expression of the dictatorship of the working class... the dictatorship of the proletariat is at the same time the dictatorship of the Communist Party." (Zinoviev, 1920)

"the State cannot be sure of its own self-preservation without an armed force to defend it . . . against the discontent of its own people." (Bakunin)

Six points in reply to Iain McKay

By Martin Thomas

URL: http://bit.ly/vpPHuf

1: "Bakunin, Kropotkin, and Malatesta were not so naive as to believe that anarchism could be established overnight..."

Certainly sometimes they wrote that the road to an anarchist society would be long. But always, as far I know, they insisted that anarchists should dispute, resist, and disrupt moves by workers to create a strong, centralised, democratic authority of their own — a workers' state or semi-state — during or after the revolutionary overthrow of the capitalist class.

In practice, during revolutions, anarchists have often supported some revolutionary power (the Paris Commune, if you count the left-Proudhonists like Varlin as anarchists; the Council of People's Commissars in November 1917). In the Spanish revolution of 1936-7, the strongest anarchist-led movement ever to exist, the CNT/ FAI, responded to the need for coordination against the counter-revolution (the fascists) by entering the bourgeois governments of Catalonia and the Spanish Republic.

In revolutionary times, anarchists must abandon their anti-government dogma, or else box themselves into inadvertently helping counter-revolution by their efforts to disrupt the creation of a revolutionary power. The trouble is that then they have no criteria as to "how much" to abandon it. If all government is bad, but you are forced by the needs of struggle against counter-revolution to recognise some government as a necessary evil, then a workers' government appears no less evil than a bourgeois-republican one, and a bourgeois-republican government no less necessary than a workers' one.

How does anarchist writers' "theoretical" line of insisting on the immediate abolition of all government in a revolution square with their admission that anarchism cannot be established overnight?

For many anarchists, and probably most anarchists today, it is not a problem. They regard anarchism as a distant ideal. Action is not gauged so as quickly to realise the ideal, but to bring it closer by pushing bit-by-bit in an anti-government direction.

There were periods, though, when Bakunin and Kropotkin were confident about early prospects of revolution. Then, they wrote of the abolition of government as something which could be achieved immediately, in the coming revolution, and which must be achieved, or else the revolution would be fruitless. They did claim that the abolition of government could be achieved "overnight", or after a brief but fruitful period of chaos.

Anarchists' ideas about revolution are less problematic when revolution is distant both in reality and, even more so, in the minds of the anarchists. They are harmful and disruptive when revolution is close. [See also McKay's sections on "Anarchism and defence of the revolution", and "Anarchism and revolution"].

2. Anarchists and working-class struggle

I wrote (*Solidarity* 195): "Some anarchists — primarily the anarcho-syndicalists, who on this issue have the same idea as Marxists do — identify with the working class as the force to defeat the capitalist state and create a new society; but most do not". For the purpose of "refuting" this statement, Iain McKay first converts it into something significantly different.

His version of what I wrote is: "Some anarchists do [support class struggle]. Those are the anarcho-syndicalists, who on this issue have the same idea as Marxists do... but most schools of anarchism do not".

I wrote "primarily" (i.e. not only) the anarcho-syndicalists. McKay has me saying that it is only the anarcho-syndicalists. I wrote that the anarcho-syndicalists and some other anarchists "identify with the working class as the force to defeat the capitalist state and create a new society", while yet other anarchists do not. McKay has me saying something different: that anarchists other than anarcho-syndicalists do not even "support class struggle".

As Yves Coleman writes in a sympathetic account of "today's young anarchists" (*Solidarity* 224): "The most 'physical'... anarchists want to confront physically the cops, to throw Molotov cocktails... etc. The more 'peaceful' ones... want to build new human relationships here and now... organising squats or communes [etc.]"

Pretty much all of them welcome unrest, strife, rebellion, strikes. No question about that. They support class struggle in that sense. But their focus is not on class struggle.

Even some anarchists who (like the Anarchist Federation) describe themselves as "class-struggle anarchists", to distinguish themselves from other anarchists, do not quite share the same view as anarcho-syndicalists or Marxists.

The AF's strategy is based on two great values: "direct action" and "self-organisation", also summed up as "a culture of resistance". The AF sympathises with the working class and favours biff and strife. But if you unpick its arguments, you see that biff is valued primarily as "direct", "self-organised", and "local", rather than primarily as working-class.

Most anarchists criticise Marxists for differentiating between the wage-working class and, on the other hand, the peasantry and the lumpenproletariat. They are sympathetic to the wage-working class, but regard the peasantry and lumpenproletariat as equally, or sometimes more, the forces for revolution.

Today in Britain, anarchism broadly defined probably has more energetic young people then the aggregate of all the would-be Trotskyist activist groups. Yet visibly the impact of anarchists in working-class struggles is less than the impact (for good, or sometimes for worse) of even one of the main would-be Trotskyist groups. That is partly because of many anarchists' distaste for systematic long-term organising beyond small "affinity groups", but partly also because of priorities.

3. Anarchism and anarcho-syndicalism

McKay then claims, or seems to claim, that almost all anarchism, at least after Bakunin, is anarcho-syndicalism anyway.

He gives a highly compressed version of a passage from Marx in which Marx seems to attribute anarcho-syndicalism to Bakunin.

McKay's version: "Bakunin's programme [is that] the working class must not occupy itself with politics. They must only organise themselves by trades-unions [and] by means of the International, they will supplant the place of all existing states".

Marx's original: "Bakunin's programme [held that] the working class must not occupy itself with politics. They must only organise themselves by trades-unions. One fine day, by means of the International, they will supplant the place of all existing states. You see what a caricature he [Bakunin] has made of my doctrines!

"As the transformation of the existing States into Associations is our last end, we must allow the governments, those great Trade-Unions of the ruling classes, to do as they like, because to occupy ourselves with them is to acknowledge them. Why! In the same way the old socialists said: You must not occupy yourselves with the wages question, because you want to abolish wages labour, and to struggle with the capitalist about the rate of wages is to acknowledge the wages system!

"The ass has not even seen that every class movement, as a class movement, is necessarily and was always a political movement".

In the disputes in the First International around 1870, Bakunin's faction, the anarchists-to-be, made opposition to political and electoral activity by the working class their point of honour. Arguing as they were from within the First International, their opposition to political activity more or less automatically defined economic and trade-union activity for them as the only road to liberation.

Some of what they wrote reads with hindsight like an early statement of the later anarcho-syndicalist idea. I think the apparent identity is an anachronistic illusion. Around 1870 trade unions everywhere were weak. Where they were strongest, in Britain, they tended more to Liberalism than to anarchism or Marxism. No-one really could or did have a short-term practical project of expanding and improving them so that they could quickly become strong enough to hollow out and throw off the capitalist state and the employing class.

Equally, it is anachronistic to read references by Bakunin and Kropotkin to "workers' associations" and so on as descriptions-in-advance of the workers' councils (soviets) which first emerged in Russia in 1905 [cf: McKay's section, "Anarchism and Workers' Councils"]. Proudhon, whom both Bakunin and Kropotkin frequently acknowledged as their teacher, had limned a future society composed of local economic cooperatives interacting through trade (on equal terms) rather than with coordination by a wider-than-local workers' authority. "Workers' associations" was a description of the basic economic and social units of the new society.

After 1872 the anarchists-to-be separated from the Marxists and, bit by bit, from the non-anarchist allies they'd had in their factional battle in the First International. Over the 1870s anarchism emerged as a distinct current in political activity (albeit one which protested that its political activity avoided politics). Nothing like anarcho-syndicalism emerged at first. For two decades, until the mid 1890s, its dominant concern was not building workers' unions, but "propaganda by the deed".

In 1895, Fernand Pelloutier wrote an article, "Anarchism and the Workers' Union", urging anarchists to plunge into the unions. His article shows a writer aware that he is arguing for a change of direction, not someone just reminding anarchists of old common-stock ideas.

The French CGT did not emerge in full form until 1902, and the Spanish CNT until 1910. With them, anarcho-syndicalism became for a while the most vigorous, though still not the only, strand of anarchism. Since the decay of the French CGT into reformist syndicalism, in the years up to 1914, and the political collapse of the CNT with the entry of the Spanish anarchists into bourgeois governments in 1936, anarcho-syndicalism has been a subordinate strand among many in anarchism.

4. Anarchism and the medieval commune

McKay quotes a couple of sentences from Bakunin, and one from Kropotkin, indicating awareness of differences between medieval communes and the Paris Commune. Those should be read together with the much greater number of sentences in which they emphasised what the commune of the future would have in common with the medieval commune of the past, both of them representing the supposed trend of human nature when freed from the unnatural constraint of an organised state machine.

5. Anarchism and capitalism

Iain McKay has written a lot against pro-capitalist individualists in the USA who claim to be anarchists. I'd happily second his wish to disqualify those right-wingers who attempt to steal a self-description used by pro-working-class, socialistic activists. I ask only that he would recognise that the "Marxists" running Stalinist states had and have even less right to steal the descriptions "communist", "Marxist", or "revolutionary socialist". (But he doesn't recognise that: see below, "equating Trotskyism with Stalinism").

McKay seems to want to claim that I equate his anarchism with those pro-capitalist individualists. I don't.

I wrote that in Bakunin's activity in the League for Peace and Freedom, in 1867-8 — probably his largest-scale activity, and the only one for which he wrote a more or less comprehensive manifesto — he "made no demand for the expropriation of capitalist property or the collective ownership of the means of production" and remonstrated that "the majority of decent, industrious bourgeois" could quite well support his programme.

McKay quotes a snippet as if I were denying that Bakunin subsequently moved to the left. I do not deny that. I wrote that Bakunin's "writings of [his first months in the First International, 1868-9] suggest that he was genuinely won over by Marx's ideas as transmitted through the International. They read as paraphrases — with a particular bias and twist, but paraphrases — of the general ideas of the International".

I quoted Proudhon from "The Philosophy of Poverty": "The net product belongs to [the man of enterprise] by the most sacred title recognised among men — labour and intelligence. It is useless to recall the fact that the net product is often exaggerated, either by fraudulently secured reductions of wages or in some other way. These are abuses... which remain outside the domain of the theory".

McKay disputes my summary comment that "Proudhon did not even see industrial capital as exploitative" by offering another quote from Proudhon talking about revenue being "confiscated by the entrepreneur".

McKay's quote also comes from "The Philosophy of Poverty". It comes between a passage in which Proudhon complains about lending at interest as apparently the prime form of exploitation, and a passage where he repeats his key idea that trade should by its essence be between equal values but due to some perversion is not: "commerce, the exchange of essentially equal values, is only the art of buying for three francs what is worth six, and selling for six francs what is worth three".

Proudhon, as Marx commented, fancied himself as a dialectician. Not only did his views change a lot over his life; even in a single book, as here in "The Philosophy of Poverty", he often contradicted himself and took pride in doing so.

The broad drift of Proudhon's thought can however be assessed from the facts that "free credit" became the hobby-horse of the Proudhonists, and that the Proudhonists formed the unsuccessful opposition in the First International to collective ownership of the means of production.

Finally, McKay quotes anarchists saying that the state protects capital as refuting my comment that the "fathers" of anarchism held that "human nature favours liberty and solidarity, the state is an artificial imposition, and capitalism is the product of the state". There is no refutation here. Bakunin and Kropotkin could quite consistently hold that the artificial imposition of the state had led to the rise of capital, and also that the state then protected capital.

6. Equating Trotskyism with Stalinism (and with social democracy?)

Much debate here started with me citing a string of words which the anarchist writers Schmidt and van der Walt "quote" as Trotsky's own description of a socialist future. I responded:

"The footnotes show that the words put in quote marks by Schmidt and van der Walt, as if they come from Trotsky, are culled not from Trotsky himself but from 'pages 128, 132' of a book by one Wayne Thorpe.

"Some of the words may have been taken by Thorpe from one of the polemics in which, in late 1920 — between the Bolsheviks' voting-down of Trotsky's first proposal in February 1920 of what would become the more liberal 'New Economic Policy' and the adoption of the NEP itself, on Lenin's initiative, in early 1921 — Trotsky sought expedients to get the economy of revolutionary Russia into working order in the midst of civil war".

75

I challenged anarchists to provide evidence that the supposed "quote" was a valid summary of Trotsky's thought. "None of the words was ever written by Trotsky as a statement of his vision of socialism. The quoted string of words was never written as a whole connected passage by Trotsky anywhere".

In the section of his sheet headed "The AWL versus Marxism", Iain McKay quotes my challenge, and fails to answer it.

He does, however, try to dispute the idea that "Trotsky fought Stalinism to the death", after first suggesting that Marx and Engels favoured a parliamentary road to socialism, using the old bourgeois state machine and only adapting it a little.

At a time when the bourgeois state machine (standing army, bureaucracy, police) in England was very flimsy compared to what it had become by the end of the 19th century, and very flimsy compared to the state machines in some other countries in Europe, Marx thought that the ballot-box might let the working class win political supremacy. The bourgeoisie thought that too, which is why it resisted the working-class campaign for voting rights, and made concessions only in small doses and in proportion as it had consolidated a state machine and secured some political hegemony over the working class. Engels later commented that Marx had thought that "England [was] the only country where the inevitable social revolution might be effected entirely by peaceful and legal means. He certainly never forgot to add that he hardly expected the English ruling classes to submit, without a 'pro-slavery rebellion', to this peaceful and legal revolution".

Maybe Marx was wrong on that. It is a reasonable subject for debate. It has nothing to do with the alleged idea of taking over the existing bureaucratic state machine and using it, only slightly modified, to bring socialism. Marx's argument, right or wrong, was not about the suitability of the bureaucratic bourgeois state machine as an instrument for socialism, but about its flimsy and lightweight character in England in a certain period, and therefore the possible greater ease of replacing it by a radically different mode of government.

McKay quotes a sentence where he has Engels saying that in Holland "only a few changes [would] have to be made to establish that free self-government by the working class". I can't trace the quote and its context (McKay gives no source), and so can give no comment.

As for Trotsky and the other Bolsheviks, there is no question about it that they organised a harsh military regime during the Civil War after the Russian Revolution, 1917-22. They did it to defend the revolution.

That they made mistakes in the maelstrom is a reasonable claim. As

Rosa Luxemburg wrote: "a model and faultless proletarian revolution in an isolated land, exhausted by world war, strangled by imperialism, betrayed by the international proletariat, would be a miracle".

Also reasonable is the claim that, in that maelstrom, the Bolsheviks sometimes elevated the exigencies or expedients of adversity into general rules. It is certain that some passages from what they wrote make that false elevation, and plausible that even taken in context those passages skew the arguments out of shape.

Not a reasonable assessment is the idea that when they made mistakes in the direction of being too brusque and too military, those mistakes stemmed from a systematic bias in Marxism and Bolshevism towards authoritarianism and undemocracy.

The Russian Marxists and Bolsheviks had fought the Tsarist state for over two decades primarily under the banners of "social democracy" and "consistent democracy". Most of them, until 1917, believed that a radical democratic revolution was the best possible outcome in Russia, and that a socialist revolution must come after a whole further development.

They had separated off from the previous radical movement in Russia, the populists, who were heavily anarchist-tinged, around two basic ideas: that formal-democratic laws and rights were worth fighting for, even short of socialism; and that the way to win them was mass self-controlling action by the workers, not conspiracies by a brave and small elite to strike down the leaders of the old regime. The urgency and importance of democratic rights were central to the cause for which they faced persecution, jail, and exile.

They also knew that no-one can go through history reading off all their actions from a pocketbook of democratic rules. They knew that civil wars require emergency measures. That their choice of emergency measures included mistakes is plausible, and in the circumstances almost certain to have been true.

A response to them which says: "Oh no! Things would have gone better if the Soviets had organised no central authority, no Red Army, no military discipline, and submitted to being slaughtered by the counter-revolutionaries with the consolation that they had proved themselves as democratic idealists" is, in effect if not in intention, an abandonment of practical revolutionary politics.

Since the first version of this book was published, Iain McKay has protested that we misrepresent him. He is (he says) accurately quoting a first-draft version of my article:

"By no means all anarchists identify with the working class as the force to defeat the capitalist state and create a new society. Some anarchists do. Those are the anarcho-syndicalists..."

He is not quoting the article as eventually published, which said:

"Some anarchists — primarily the anarcho-syndicalists... — identify with the working class as the force to defeat the capitalist state and create a new society; but most do not".

However:

1. To build your polemic on a first draft, rather than the corrected and published version which came out very soon after it, is shoddy.

2. To make a big issue of the difference between the more careful wording "primarily anarcho-syndicalists" and the cruder first-draft version, "anarcho-syndicalists" is odd from Iain. He argues that pretty much all anarchists were at least incipiently "anarcho-syndicalists" even long before the term "anarcho-syndicalist" emerged. To him there is no sharp division between anarcho-syndicalists and other anarchists. Therefore, there can be no sharp division between the formulations "some anarchists, i.e. anarcho-syndicalists", and "some anarchists, primarily anarcho-syndicalists but also others".

3. The main problem with Iain's way of quoting me on this point is that he has me claiming that among anarchists only anarcho-syndicalists (or, only some anarchists, primarily anarcho-syndicalists but also others) *support working-class struggle.*

That is not what I claimed. I pointed out, for example, that "Bakunin supported unions and strikes", yet "did not see the working class as the central agent of revolution".

All or almost anarchists today generally support rebellion and resistance by the disadvantaged, including the working class. That is an important point of common ground. But it is not the same as identifying the cause of socialist revolution with the wage-working class, as distinct from the oppressed in general.

MT

Working-class struggle and anarchism: a debate

By Martin Thomas

This first article, originally published in *Solidarity* 195, 2 March 2011, sparked a lengthy online debate, which we are only able to reproduce short excerpts from here. To read the whole debate, including lengthy contributions from anarchist writers attacking the article and the AWL, see the URL below. Martin Thomas's reply to the debate, along with the excerpts from Iain McKay and Dee, appeared in *Solidarity* 196, 9 March 2011.

URL: www.workersliberty.org/anarch1

Anarchism opposes the capitalist state. Some anarchists — primarily the anarcho-syndicalists, who on this issue have the same idea as Marxists do — identify with the working class as the force to defeat the capitalist state and create a new society; but most do not.

Pierre-Joseph Proudhon, the "father of anarchism", was opposed to unions, strikes, and class struggle. "We...wage war", he wrote, "not upon the rich but upon principles... We are socialists, not despoilers... men of reconciliation and progress".

He condemned the press for supporting workers' strikes for better wages. "It is impossible for strikes followed by an increase of wages to end otherwise than in a general rise of prices... The working men, supported by the favour of an indiscreet press, in demanding an increase of wages, have served monopoly much better than their own real interests".

He did not even see industrial capital as exploitative. In his view only financial and merchant capital were exploitative.

He seized upon a lull in trade-union activity in Britain to exclaim: "The British workers have got out of the habit of combination, which is assuredly a progress for which one cannot but congratulate them".

Proudhon is credited with coining the phrase later popularised by Marx, that the emancipation of the working class must be the task of the workers themselves. At any rate Proudhon wrote in 1848 that "the proletariat must emancipate itself without the help of the government".

But Proudhon did not mean emancipation through class struggle. He meant that the workers should organise themselves into small workshop groups and trade between the groups. He claimed that by doing that "they would soon have wrested alienated capital back again... become the masters of it all... without the proprietors being despoiled..."

By the time that Mikhail Bakunin became the leading writer of anarchism, in the 1870s, working-class struggle was strong enough to make Bakunin support unions and strikes. Bakunin still (like Proudhon) opposed workers organising into a workers' political party.

He did not see the working class as the central agent of revolution. He considered peasants and the urban unemployed, beggars, petty criminals, etc. to be much more potent revolutionary forces.

Today, anarchists identifying with Zapatismo accept the Zapatistas' strategic decision to orient to the peasants of Chiapas, an economically little-developed region in the south of Mexico, rather than the workers in Mexico's huge cities. "Autonomists", in practice close to anarchism though their ideas originate from Marxist discussions, hold that the agency for change is now no longer the working class, but the "multitude". By "refusal, desertion, exodus and nomadism", the "multitude" can produce "a kind of spontaneous and elementary communism".

Revolutionary activity, for them, is not about class struggle, but about "the affirmation of the movement itself as an 'alternative society'... To conquer and control its own 'spaces'...".

The contemporary "social-ecology" anarchist writer Murray Bookchin insists that "we are no longer living in a world where revolutionary consciousness can be developed primarily or even significantly around the issue of wage-labour versus capital". Instead, "the revolutionary project" must be "a counter-culture".

The working class, he complains, expresses not universal human interests but "bourgeois egoism". "Anarchist theories and movements" are linked by an "umbilical cord" to "organic societies... the clan, tribe, polis, medieval commune... the village and decentralised towns of the past".

How Bookchin thinks that such an unpromising society as capitalism, with the majority of the population belonging to the proletariat, "the most inorganic of all oppressed classes", can generate a "counter-culture" except as marginal, is not clear. In practice, many anarchists pursue the day-to-day business of "counter-cultural" activity as an end in itself, and the final aim remains in the blurred distance.

PREPARATION

It is no part of Marxism to deny the value of imaginative "stunts". But we do believe that revolutionaries must prepare for revolution by a focus on patient, long-term work in working-class struggles (even small ones).

The wage-working class in capitalist society has a twofold character. It is both the basic alienated class, having its life reduced to the margins around a process of labour for capital which sucks out its energy while returning to it only a pittance by which to keep its labour-power in trim; and the basic creative class, developing an ever-more-multifarious cooperative potency in production.

Capitalist production throws the working class into constant conflicts with capital over the terms and conditions of the sale of labour-power. Even if limited to the issue of wages, those battles generate class organisations of the workers — trade unions — and ties of class solidarity. Extended to issues of workers' control over production, they pose the question of the principle of solidarity replacing the rules of the market.

A cooperative commonwealth is not just a benevolent scheme to relieve the sufferings of the workers. It is the photographic positive for which the negative is provided by the struggle of the working class, within capitalist society, to lift the burdens of its class subordination by abolishing it.

In opposition to the Marxist view, focused on long-term organising, activists can be drawn to anarchism today by either one of two apparently contradictory impulses: the desire for immediately "revolutionary" activity, or the resigned conclusion that revolution is so remote that the best we can do for now is to poke at the capitalist order piecemeal but in the most colourful way we can find.

Anarchists know as well as Marxists do that only a minority in normal times are consistently active. But anarchists — again with the exception of anarcho-syndicalists — lack a coherent idea of how the minority can act today so as best to contribute to majority action tomorrow.

ANARCHO-SYNDICALISM

Anarcho-syndicalism is the version of anarchism that identifies the society of the future as a federation of industries each run by the trade-union of the workers in the industry, rather than as federation of small local communes.

Unlike other variants of anarchism, anarcho-syndicalism focuses on the wage-working class. It has a coherent idea of what to do in un-revolutionary times: build up the unions which will later be the instruments of revolution.

Anarcho-syndicalism is far from "pure" anarchism, where the axis is the small local autonomous group (or even individuals) against (any) state, rather than workers against capital. Arguing with fellow anarchists to turn away from their closed discussion circles and small bomb-throwing conspiracies towards the unions, Fernand Pelloutier, the pioneer of French anarcho-syndicalism (which was a mass movement between 1902 and 1914) wrote that:

"Nobody believes or expects that the coming revolution will realise unadulterated anarchist communism". Trade-union administration of society would be the best "transitional state" available.

Weren't the trade unions disciplined, collective bodies? Didn't that outrage the individualist sensibilities of anarchism? Well, said Pelloutier, in unions "individuals are at liberty to quit, except... when battle has been joined with the enemy". Presumably he hoped that anarchists would overlook how big an "except" that was...

Inside the mass French trade-union movement, the CGT, the determined revolutionary syndicalists formed a self-conscious "active minority", mostly grouped around newspapers and magazines, who deliberately strove to educate rather than just to rely on spontaneous rebellion.

Trotsky described that French revolutionary syndicalism as "a remarkable draft outline of revolutionary communism".

Unfortunately, most anarchists today are not anarcho-syndicalists. When there is a big workers' struggle, the people contributing support and proposals, organising rank-and-file groups, and so on, are mostly (for better or for worse) the various Marxist or would-be Marxist groups, not anarchist groups. And the anarcho-syndicalist "draft outline" was and is lacking in several respects.

Firstly, in anarcho-syndicalist perspectives the unions have to combine the three distinct roles played in a Marxist perspective by three distinct sorts of organisation — the workers' political party (or proto-party), the unions, and the workers' councils.

The result is a sort of pantomime-horse effect. Unions, if they are to be effective, must include as nearly as possible the whole workforce, excluding only strike-breakers. Under anywhere near normal conditions, they include many workers whose social ideas are conformist and bourgeois.

To try to make the union a revolutionary-educational force is to narrow it down and make it ineffective as a union. The activists end up with neither an effective union, nor an effective party, but something which is botched in both respects. The French revolutionary-syndicalist idea of "the active minority" was a partial answer, but only a partial one, to that problem.

Further, even the broadest unions usually organise only a minority of the workforce. Usually the worst-off sections of the working class are not, or only scantily, unionised. In revolutionary times, those worst-off sections explode into activity. Workers then need much broader and more flexible organisations than even the trade unions — namely, workers' councils.

Those workers' councils will be the foundation of the future workers' state. It should be the unions instead? But if the unions are to play the role of rulers in the future society, then what will play the role of unions? Even under a workers' state, individual groups of workers may sometimes need to assert their particular interests against the collective.

Although, as Pelloutier admitted, the anarcho-syndicalists effectively abandoned the "pure anarchist" idea of immediate abolition of all government, they did keep warning the workers against what Emile Pouget, another leader of the CGT, called "the virus of politics".

The warnings could not stop the "virus" spreading. Politics abhors a vacuum.. Despite the CGT's calls not to vote, most CGT workers voted socialist... and for socialists who in their majority turned out to be unprincipled parliamentary reformists — since anarcho-syndicalist doctrine banned the more revolutionary activists from using the electoral arena for their own agitational, educational, recruitment efforts.

Syndicalism cannot be equated fully with "economism". Around the end of the 19th century, a section of the Russian Marxists, bowled over by the success of their new agitation on workplace economic issues, came to argue that socialists should focus exclusively or overwhelmingly on such economic issues, leaving outside-the-workplace political issues to the bourgeois liberals for the time being, and that socialist politics would then easily grow out of the extension of economic struggle. That was "economism".

The CGT put much effort into political campaigns against militarism, and indeed explicitly against "patriotism". That makes its collapse into supporting the French government in 1914 all the more revealing of the ultimate inadequacy of its strategy.

The syndicalists were not quite "economists". But they curtailed their political agitation by their belief that strong union organisation was ultimately enough, by itself, to make a revolution; and by their fear of the "virus of politics".

They could campaign against reactionary government measures — in 1913, the CGT established a united front with the Socialist Party, to protest against the government introducing a three-year term of compulsory military service — but they could never campaign for positive reforms to be nailed down in law! They could not campaign for votes for women, for example, because their principle was to avoid and reject voting for parliament. All their political activity was done with one hand tied behind their backs.

STATE

As Trotsky pointed out: "By the manner in which they treat the question [of the state], the syndicalists, unwittingly of course, contribute to the passive conciliation of the workers with the capitalist state.

"When the syndicalists keep drumming into the workers, who are oppressed by the bourgeois state, their warnings about the dangers of a proletarian state, they play a purely reactionary role.

"The bourgeois will readily repeat to the workers: 'Do not touch the state because it is a snare full of dangers to you'..."

The anarcho-syndicalists had no real idea of how to deal with the bourgeois state, other than the thought that if they could organise a full general strike then bourgeois power would simply collapse. They took great comfort in calculations that compared the numbers of the French army with the length of railway line in France, and concluded that in a perfect general strike the army could not exert control over the railways, let alone over any other industry.

In reality, such a perfect general strike is impossible. Faced with World War One in 1914, the syndicalists knew that their cure-all of a general strike to stop war was impractical. While revolutionary Marxists like Lenin and Luxemburg, who had always rejected the anarchist myth of the perfect general strike, were able to start organising opposition to the war, the CGT collapsed into support for its own government in the war no less abjectly than the parliamentary-reformist socialists.

Only a minority among the syndicalists, people like Alfred Rosmer and Pierre Monatte, remained true to their principles. And in the course of doing so, they found that they had to develop their principles, and become "political" revolutionary communists, Marxists.

THE ROMANTIC VIEWPOINT

Marx wrote: "In bourgeois economics — and in the epoch of production to which it corresponds — this complete working-out of the human content [by ever-expanding, ever-more-diverse production] appears as a complete emptying-out, this universal objectification as total alienation, and the tearing-down of all limited, one-sided aims as sacrifice of the human end-in-itself to an entirely external end..."

Only, Marx argues that the working class can and must press forward, through this "working-out", to overthrowing capital and creating the free association of producers on an extensive and rich rather than a localised and poor basis.

"The mass of workers must themselves appropriate their own surplus labour. Once they have done so — and disposable time thereby ceases to have an antithetical existence — then, on one side, necessary labour time will be measured by the needs of the social individual, and, on the other, the development of the power of social production will grow so rapidly that... disposable time will grow for all. For real wealth is the developed productive power of all individuals. The measure of wealth is then not any longer, in any way, labour time, but rather disposable time".

"It is as ridiculous", writes Marx, "to yearn for a return to [the] original fullness as it is to believe that with this complete emptiness history has come to a standstill. The bourgeois viewpoint has never advanced beyond this antithesis between itself and this romantic viewpoint, and therefore the latter will accompany it as legitimate antithesis up to its blessed end".

Anarchism — with the exception of anarcho-syndicalism — is essentially a variant of the "romantic viewpoint".

NESTOR MAKHNO

David Footman, in his book *Civil War in Russia*, describes the efforts in 1917-21 of the peasant army led by Nestor Makhno. The "Makhnovshchina" was arguably the largest-scale effort ever made actually to run a significant area on anarchist lines.

Most of the "theoretical" anarchists who joined Makhno quickly quit when they saw that the necessities of battle had brought him to the same wartime expedients which they had damned as "authoritarian Marxism" when employed by the Bolsheviks: military orders, conscription, food requisitions, secret police, summary assassination of opponents (which, for Makhno, most of the time, included Bolsheviks).

Yet Makhno was a serious man of ideas, and had real support among peasants. As Footman records, "Many of [the Makhnovites'] ideas made sense to Ukrainian peasants whose one political obsession was to be rid of any outside interference. Most of their ideas make nonsense when applied to any larger or more developed administrative unit".

The Makhno movement had no idea how to organise towns. It airily told workers concerned at the fact that they had not received wages and had no food to "organise a free economic order from below". At the two workers' conferences which the Makhnovites organised in the area they controlled in October 1919, the big majority of the workers were hostile to the Makhnovites.

To peasants, or small-scale craft workers, used to living their whole lives in small collectives, it can make sense that the small collective should manage its own affairs and deal with whatever it needs from outside its area by ad hoc contracts with other similar collectives.

To the modern wage-worker, used to living in large cities, to moving from job to job and city to city, and conscious that her or his job is part of an enormously ramified chain of production, it makes no sense.

THE MURMURED ALTERNATIVE

The constant whirl of capitalist restructuring implies also a constant whirl of breaking-up and sidelining workers' organisations as they exist at any given time. The organisation constantly requires rebuilding. After a series of defeats, it may stumble at a low level for a long time.

And it may need to be rebuilt in a form seriously different from what it had before the defeats. After the Chartist movement of the British workers in the 1830s and 1840s, and the mostly short-lived trade union organisations associated with it, were defeated, for a long time attempts to organise a revival came to nothing. When the working-class revival came in the 1880s, its form — the New Unionism, mostly in large-scale industry, and the first Marxist groups — was significantly different from that of 1830s and 1840s.

But, so long as capital continues, the workers' movement will rebuild, and its rebuilding will include trade-union organisation, even though we cannot predict the specific forms and tempos.

While the workers' movement remains at a low level, it cannot overthrow capital and make a revolution. But nor can anyone else. The revolutionaries need to decide what long-term work they can do, in relatively quiet times and (if the revolutionaries are not very numerous) on a small scale, which will best prepare the way for mass revolutionary action in the future.

In September 1850 Marx decided that he and his comrades faced a long period when the workers' movement would be at a low level. He broke with the majority of the Communist League exiles in London, with these words:

"We tell the workers: If you want to change conditions and make yourselves capable of government, you will have to undergo fifteen, twenty or fifty years of civil war.

"Now they are told [by the majority]: We must come to power immediately or we might as well go to sleep. The word proletariat' has been reduced to a mere phrase, like the word 'people' was by the democrats.

"To make this phrase a reality one would have to declare the entire petty bourgeois to be proletarians, i.e. de facto represent the petty bourgeoisie and not the proletariat. In place of actual revolutionary development one would have to adopt the revolutionary phrase".

Only by a lengthy development within capitalist society (by civil war, Marx evidently means social war, rather than necessarily military battle), does the working class become the revolutionary working class.

To adopt the "revolutionary phrase", that is, to pretend that conditions are always immediately revolutionary, is to end up recommending whatever oppositional movements, or even just protest activities, are immediately to hand, and glossing them up as more than they are, rather than cleaving to the long-term interests of the working class.

Antonio Negri once expressed well a basic idea of Marxism. "The fact that we cannot spell out the alternative does not necessarily mean that it does not exist. It exists as a murmuring among the proletariat".

Marxist tactics are about organising ourselves to hear and listen to that "murmuring among the proletariat", to develop dialogue with it, and by dialogue to raise it first to open speech and then finally to a yell of victory.

Bakunin and Proudhon unfairly maligned

By Iain McKay (excerpt)

"[Proudhon] did not even see industrial capital as exploitative. In his view only financial and merchant capital were exploitative".

Not remotely true — Proudhon was quite explicit that exploitation was a product of wage-labour, of workers selling their labour/liberty to a boss, that it happened in production. Indeed, his theory of why industrial capital is exploitative is similar to Marx's — except that Proudhon argued it first.

Only someone utterly ignorant of Proudhon's ideas would make such a statement — I guess that they have been spending too much time reading *The Poverty of Philosophy* rather than Proudhon!

And, let us be honest, there are very, very few mutualists around — invoking Proudhon is irrelevant because most anarchists are revolutionaries, not reformists! But I guess it sets the tone for what comes next.

"Bakunin did not see the working class as the central agent of revolution. He considered peasants and the urban unemployed, beggars, petty criminals, etc. to be much more potent revolutionary forces".

Absolute nonsense...

Anarchists are class-struggle people

By Dee (excerpt)

Just as not every self-styled socialist can actually be considered a socialist — so too it is with anarchism. See for example, "Black Flame: The Revolutionary Class Politics of Anarchism and Syndicalism", which argues with some evidence that the only type of anarchism is class struggle anarchism — hence Proudhon, Bookchin, as well as primitivist, individualist, utopian "anarchists" cannot be considered anarchist.

"Pierre-Joseph Proudhon, the 'father of anarchism', was opposed to unions, strikes, and class struggle". Right, given that his ideas on unions, strikes and class struggle (or any of his ridiculous petty-bourgeois mutualist ideas) have literally zero sway in contemporary anarchist thought, the relevance of this is...?

For what it's worth, in anarchist circles I've been involved with, the only ideas of Proudhon's given any notice are his ideas on surplus value

— ideas which Marx (who, in the opinion of almost every anarchist I've met, is an infinitely better thinker and more useful and closer to our politics than Proudhon) was massively influenced by.

"Bakunin did not see the working class as the central agent of revolution. He considered peasants and the urban unemployed, beggars, petty criminals, etc. to be much more potent revolutionary forces."

You're going for the classic "anarchists only care about peasants" line. I didn't realise that was still used against anarchists for real. You've got Bakunin wrong, as it happens. Having said that, I don't know a single living anarchist who bases their ideas on his...

Why write a massive load on anarchist politics that have no modern sway? In doing so you make anarcho-syndicalism (and all other types of class struggle anarchism, which don't seem to exist for you...) sound marginal — when actually the vast majority of anarchists and anarchist struggles have been class struggle in nature.

You do it to malign anarchism, and that is the purpose of this essay, there is no honest intent to it.

A response to the polemics

By Martin Thomas

The polemicists have invoked the Anarchist Federation as proof that my criticisms of anarchism in *Solidarity* 3/195 were unjust. Let's see what the Anarchist Federation says.

Its website recommends an interview with an AF member which says:

"Too often the anarchist scene is incredibly elitist. There are loads of friendship groups doing things that exclude the participation of working-class people. They have no structures that allow people to join them, no internal democracy that places everyone on an equal footing. No point of contact for people new to anarchism. And ultimately no staying power".

This is the AF itself, describing what most anarchist activity is like. (The AF, whatever its virtues, is a tiny minority among self-described "anarchists").

It's a harsher description than I made! And I stressed in the article that some anarchists are different. Some anarchists gear their activity to working-class struggle as Marxists do. They cannot justly be condemned "by association" with the other anarchists, and I did not try to condemn them that way.

One reason for writing the article is that on many issues we find some anarchists much closer to us, that is, much more oriented to an independent working-class standpoint, than many would-be Marxists and Trotskyists. We share with class-struggle anarchists an emphasis on rank-and-file organising (against an orientation to the "left" bureaucracies in the labour movement) and a rejection of the Stalinoid organisational norms still common on the left.

Like many class-struggle anarchists, we emphasise the struggles of those elements of the working class — undocumented and precarious workers, for example — often ignored by the mainstream labour movement. And on international issues, our perspective has more in common with the focus on international working-class solidarity of most class-struggle anarchists than it does with the "Trotskyists" who orient to Hamas or Hezbollah or the Muslim Brotherhood on grounds of supposed "anti-imperialism".

SYNDICALISTS

In my *Solidarity* 3/195 article I stated that one sort of anarchists — anarcho-syndicalists — "focus on the wage-working class" and have a "coherent idea of what to do in un-revolutionary times". They have ongoing, structured organisation.

But, I argued, anarcho-syndicalists' dogmas constrain them to do their "political activity... with one hand tied behind their backs" and they conflate "the three distinct roles played in a Marxist perspective by three distinct sorts of organisation — the workers' political party (or proto-party), the unions, and the workers' councils".

There's been no comment on that criticism of anarcho-syndicalism. But some writers denounce my article on the grounds that there are variants of class-struggle anarchism other than anarcho-syndicalism. They say my article amounted to smearing non-syndicalist class-struggle anarchism by lumping it together with liberal or lifestyle-ist or utopian anarchism.

They have a fair point against the draft version of my article, which I posted on the web and which attracted the comment. In the final printed version, which I'd worked on more carefully, I wrote: "Some anarchists — primarily the anarcho-syndicalists, who on this issue have the same idea as Marxists do — identify with the working class as the force to defeat the capitalist state..." Primarily the anarcho-syndicalists; not exclusively the anarcho-syndicalists. I think "primarily" is right, and I'll explain why in the course of this response.

"Dee" asserts that my critical comments on writers in the historic tradition of anarchism, Proudhon, Bakunin, Bookchin, etc., are malicious and arbitrary smears on today's anarchists, because those writers have "no modern sway".

Others respond in a contrary way, by arguing that Proudhon, Bakunin, etc. did focus on working-class struggle.

Anarchists polemicising with Trotskyists often concern themselves heavily with history — Trotskyists are damned because of what Trotsky did about Kronstadt in March 1921, or what he said in the Bolsheviks' "trade-union debate" in late 1920 — but plainly many anarchists today think that critical comments on Proudhon or Bakunin are just irrelevant point-scoring, because "no-one thinks that today".

Our view, which we apply to our own tradition as well as to the anarchist tradition, is that everyone's thought is heavily shaped by environment and tradition. As Keynes put it: "Practical men, who believe themselves to be quite exempt from any intellectual influence, are usually the slaves of some defunct economist."

We can hope to escape being overwhelmed by the ideological influences around us — either directly, or indirectly, by forming our ideas by knee-jerk reaction — only by learning from an independent tradition which we study thoroughly and critically. We identify with the "Third Camp" Trotskyism of the Workers' Party and the Independent Socialist League, and yet we argue that both Shachtman and Draper got some things seriously wrong.

We call ourselves Trotskyists and we think Trotsky was wrong to hold to the characterisation of the USSR as a "degenerated workers' state" in the 1930s. We call ourselves Marxists, and many of us think Marx was wrong, for example, on the "tendency of the rate of profit to fall".

We pore over the history because we believe, like Isaac Newton, that if we can see anything clearly it is because we stand on the shoulders of giants.

It's the same reason why Marx spent so much effort unpicking the ideas of Feuerbach, Proudhon, Ricardo, and others, the people who for him were what Isaac Barrow was for Newton.

When we discuss other schools of thought — like anarchism — we have the same approach. We take the ideas seriously. We dig through the history. It is not gratuitous.

It could make sense to use Kropotkin's term "anarchist communism" for your politics, while criticising Kropotkin on some issues — say, his support for World War One — and analysing how your criticisms relate to the core of Kropotkin's ideas. But to us it makes no sense to say airily that the whole history of your own tradition is irrelevant because it has "no modern sway".

PROUDHON

Iain McKay takes the contrary tack: he defends Proudhon and the rest of the traditional anarchist writers as champions of working-class struggle.

That Kropotkin generally sympathised with "the people" and even with "the workers", I don't doubt. That "Bakunin supported unions and strikes" I wrote in so many words.

Proudhon's statement that "the proletariat must emancipate itself without the help of the government" I quoted deliberately, so as to give the strongest evidence for the claim that Proudhon saw working-class struggle as the lever of change.

My argument was not that most anarchists fail to see working-class struggles as good examples of the "direct action" by "self-organised groups" against large-scale authority which they favour. It was that anarchism, where "the axis is the small local autonomous group (or even individuals) against (any) state, rather than workers against capital", is constitutionally less able than Marxism to find a way that "the minority can act today so as best to contribute to majority action tomorrow [which can replace capitalism]".

It is logical and a flaw, not an aberration and not a virtue, that most (not all) anarchists prefer "affinity" groups and one-off actions to ongoing organisation structured around definite political ideas.

In The Philosophy of Poverty — yes, I have read it, and not just Marx's polemic against it — Proudhon writes of "liberty", "equality", "association", "solidarity", and even of "a war of labour against capital".

Proudhon wishes well for the workers, in general. But he opposes strikes. His characteristic stance is that of the "man of science" pointing the way forward to be achieved by people in general understanding his enlightened views.

He seems to me to have the not-uncommon disdain of the self-consciously brainy self-educated skilled worker (which is what he was, though in later life he owned his own business and then worked as a manager) for the "average" worker.

"The day labourer has judged himself: he is content, provided he has bread, a pallet to sleep on, and plenty of liquor on Sunday. Any other condition would be prejudicial to him, and would endanger public order..."

Dockers he describes as grossly overpaid, "drunken, dissolute, brutal, insolent, selfish, and base". "One of the first reforms to be effected among the working classes will be the reduction of the wages of some at the same time that we raise those of others".

As for the rank and file in his own trade: "There are few men so weak-minded, so unlettered, as the mass of workers who follow the various branches of the typographic industry". (And, for the anti-feminist Proudhon, even worse! "The employment of women has struck this noble industry to the heart, and consummated its degradation").

He explains industrial profit as exclusively what mainstream economists would later call "pioneer's profit" and "reward for risk". "The net product belongs to [the man of enterprise] by the most sacred title recognised among men — labour and intelligence. It is useless to recall the fact that the net product is often exaggerated, either by fraudulently secured reductions of wages or in some other way. These are abuses... which remain outside the domain of the theory".

As Daniel Guérin, a sympathetic commentator on Bakunin, puts it: "It was quite unjustly, reckoned Bakunin, that Marx and Engels spoke with the greatest distrust of the lumpenproletariat, of the slum proletariat, 'for it is in it and in it alone, and not in the bourgeoisified layers of the worker masses, that the spirit and the force of the future revolution resides'."

In relation to Bakunin, "Dee" accuses me of "going for the classic 'anarchists only care about peasants' line". Where does he get that from? Anarchists, Bakunin included, tend not to differentiate much between peasants and the urban poor; the Zapatistas (not anarchists, but admired by many anarchists) are peasant-oriented; so was Makhno; so were the Russian Bakuninists when Plekhanov was their leading figure, before he became a Marxist.

But Bakunin saw the urban poor as the people most likely to organise spectacular, disruptive, localised "direct action" of the sort he considered most destructive to "authority". Of course! Only, that's different from having a strategy based on the material tendencies of capitalism and the specifically working-class struggles generated within it.

When Kropotkin came to write concise expositions of anarchism, he defined the driving force as the resurgence of a natural human order blocked only temporarily by the historical aberration of the State, and showing itself again in the way that "voluntary societies invade everything and are only impeded in their development by the State". (A sort of left-wing version of David Cameron's "Big Society").

When young people call themselves "anarchist", often all they mean is that they are left-wing but not yet sufficiently convinced to commit themselves to regular activity, instead preferring to join "actions" from time to time, or to gear their activity into a friendship group rather than a spelled-out strategy.

They have not studied Proudhon or Bakunin or Kropotkin. But those writers' focus on the small local group against authority in general, filtered through anarchist culture over the decades, is surely what makes the label "anarchist" attractive to them.

The Anarchist Federation is as critical of that sort of loose anarchism as we are. So, what of AF anarchism?

The interview quoted above is recommended by the AF website to the reader who wants "to find out more about the kinds of things AF members get up to".

"We're working heavily on the anti-ID campaign... The London comrades [do mainly admin and journalistic stuff but] somehow they find time to go on the streets and do solidarity actions too! Some of our members are busy setting up or sustaining social centres. Others are busy in their local IWW branches. Then of course there's asylum-seeker support..."

All good stuff, and all in broad terms "class struggle" activity. It differs from what the AWL does in its balance — in that we focus mainly on organising in workplaces and unions, and on self-education and the education of those around us. But that difference in focus is largely what my original article was about.

The bit of AF activity specifically focused on long-term working-class organisation (as distinct from more generic "the-people-against-power" stuff) is work in the IWW, a syndicalist organisation, suggesting that I wasn't wrong to identify anarcho-syndicalism as the "primary" form of worker-focused anarchism.

The AF's "Introduction to Anarchist Communism" extolls working-class struggle at length. But how does working-class struggle fit into AF strategy? And when the AF extolls working-class struggle, is that a roundabout way of extolling "direct action" in general, or a focus on the class character of struggle? That is less clear.

The AF states that the future society will be run by "local collectives and councils". The AF pushes two things as the means for those "local collectives" to get strong enough to organise society: "direct action" and "self-organisation", also summed up as "a culture of resistance".

"Self-organised groups" are defined as those in which "everyone has an equal say and no one is given the right to represent anyone else. This kind of group is capable of deciding its own needs and taking direct action to meet them in a way that any hierarchical group based on representatives — like a political party or a trade union — cannot".

No representatives. Not even the most democratically-elected and accountable representatives. So, the groups must indeed be "local". Very local. It is hard to see how on the AF's criteria even the workers of a single large factory could become a "self-organised group". Even anarcho-syndicalist unions have not been able to do without elected delegates, committees, secretaries, stewards, and so on. (The AF praises workers' councils as they they have existed in history, but makes no comment on the fact that these have been councils of... representatives).

How will the "local collectives" coordinate — as they must in any future society unless it is to try to reverse the development of productive forces within capitalism, which long ago went long beyond not only the small-workshop scale but even the national scale? Maybe the AF relies on Kropotkin's argument that a natural human propensity to cooperate will solve the problem. I don't know.

UNIONS

The anarcho-syndicalists, at the cost of some disrespect to anarchist dogma, had an answer to the question of coordination. Revolutionary unions — organising, through representative structures, far wider than locally — would do it.

Beyond doubt the AF, like Bakunin and Kropotkin, sympathises with the working class and favours biff and strife. And, because of anarcho-syndicalist influence I'd guess, it uses the term "working-class struggle" more than Bakunin or Kropotkin. But if you unpick the argument, you see that biff is valued primarily as "direct", "self-organised", and "local", rather than primarily as working-class.

Indeed, Marxists see struggle as "class" in character partly to the extent that it goes beyond the "local" and the immediately "self-organised". Logically, anarcho-syndicalists have, or should have, the same perception.

The AF's strategic focus on working-class struggle is qualitatively less clear than that of anarcho-syndicalists.

The critics accuse me of conflating anarcho-syndicalism and revolutionary syndicalism.

In my article, I argued that anarcho-syndicalism was the most Marxist-influenced strand of anarchism; and, in my view, Trotsky was right to describe revolutionary syndicalism in its great days as "a remarkable rough draft of revolutionary communism" (i.e. revolutionary syndicalism also influenced Bolshevik Marxism as it developed after 1917).

The spectrum of revolutionary syndicalism ranges from variants of anarchism more attentive to working-class struggle, but still fundamentally geared to a
"spontaneous-local-group-versus-structured-central-authority" axis of thinking, through to politics only a shade different from revolutionary Marxism.

Revolutionary syndicalism is, so to speak, a "transitional" political category. I think the history bears out that view.

I believe that the term "anarcho-syndicalism" was (like many other labels in politics) first coined as a pejorative term by opponents — in France in the early 1920s, by Marxists (many of them former revolutionary syndicalists who had not abjured their past, but had moved on) in their battles against the "pure" revolutionary syndicalists inside the CGTU (the more left-wing union federation, formed by expulsion from the reformist-syndicalist CGT).

In the great days of revolutionary syndicalism, before 1914, in France (the CGT) and the USA (the IWW), there was a range of views. Daniel De Leon was a sort of "Marxist-syndicalist". He took up syndicalists' ideas about transforming the trade-union movement on the basis of its elemental struggles but insisted that such activity must be coupled with "political" party activity (so far, so good, I think; but he had not yet worked out how to integrate the two wings of his strategy fully). There were anarchists in the IWW, but most leading members were not anarchists. Many had a diluted version of De Leon's scheme, being members of both the IWW and the Socialist Party but without fully integrating the two dimensions.

There were similar people in the CGT. Victor Griffuelhes, general secretary of the revolutionary syndicalist CGT in its great days, was a member of the Socialist Party (of its "Blanquist" faction). But two of the main writers of the CGT, Fernand Pelloutier and Emile Pouget, were anarchists. Pelloutier was also influenced by Marxism, having been an organised Marxist before he became an anarchist.

Some of my critics claim that anarcho-syndicalism can be sharply differentiated from revolutionary syndicalism; but historically it usually hasn't been, and some anarchists claim revolutionary syndicalism as their own. Iain McKay, in his "Anarchist FAQ", argues of "Bakunin and Kropotkin... that many of their ideas were identical to those of revolutionary syndicalism".

To the (varying, and never total) extent that it stresses "direct action" above longer-term organising and education and shies away from "politics", revolutionary syndicalism connects to anarchism. But revolutionary syndicalism of any sort inevitably involves some shift away from "pure" anarchism. How big that shift can be, and yet you still call yourself an "anarcho-syndicalist", depends I think more on fashion and personal taste than any rigid demarcation.

By crediting anarcho-syndicalism, in my original article, with all the virtues of revolutionary syndicalism, I was giving anarcho-syndicalism its strongest case, before criticising it. I was doing the very opposite of smearing it by false association.

The experience of Spanish anarcho-syndicalism — and its leaders' decision to join the bourgeois Republican governments during the Spanish Civil War — is well-trodden ground in debates between Marxists and anarchists. That's why I essayed a new angle, referring to France instead.

But Spain is relevant to the "Isaac Barrow" question.

The AF "Introduction" has a page extolling the virtues of the Spanish anarcho-syndicalists in the 1930s. What about them joining the Barcelona and Madrid bourgeois governments? The AF refers to that in passing as a "mistake".

Just that — a "mistake", as if they'd dialled a wrong digit when making a phone call. No discussion of why the "mistake" was made and what should be learned from it.

Rudolf Rocker wrote a pamphlet about Spain at the time. He didn't comment on the anarchists joining the government, but focused only on defending them against Stalinist smears. Murray Bookchin wrote a full-scale article looking back at Spain. Mainly he tells us that he finds the Spanish anarchists "admirable". He, too, suggests that joining the bourgeois governments was a mistake, but without conclusions.

Where will I find a rigorous anarchist critique of Proudhon or Bakunin? Bakunin described his ideas as "Proudhonism, extensively expanded upon and taken to its logical consequences", but quietly dropped Proudhon's opposition to unions and strikes without any full critique. Kropotkin wrote surveys of the evolution of anarchist thought, but presenting it as a bland progress, with no real polemic. And so, I think, it goes on.

Anarchists do not go much for criticising their comrades rigorously. They often spray venom at Marxists, from a distance, and they sometimes criticise their own: I've quoted the AF criticising anti-organisation anarchists; Malatesta did the same; and Bookchin wrote criticisms of different strands of anarchism. But developed polemic is rare. Although, as far as I can make out, the cult of "consensus decision-making" comes more from Quakers and capitalist management-expert advocates of "ringiseido" than from anywhere on the left, some anarchists today have adopted it as a point of honour.

As the sympathetic Daniel Guérin puts it: "The traits of anarchism are difficult to circumscribe. Its masters have almost never condensed their thought into systematic treatises... Libertarians [are] particularly inclined to swear by 'anti-dogmatism'... Anarchism is, above all, what you might call a gut revolt..."

But "don't polemicise against those you work with" tends to mean also: don't work with those who polemicise. Even the most considered critic, "Dee", declares that he'll find it "very difficult to work with AWL members" unless they disavow my article's criticisms.

Trotskyists are often accused of sectarianism and factionalism. Yet no AWL member would shy away from working in an anti-cuts committee or a stewards' committee or a union caucus with SWPers or SPers — or Labour loyalists, or anarchists — on the grounds that those groups make polemics against us much ruder than mine against anarchism!

We take it for granted that political and polemical differ by only two letters...

Anarchists don't. That is why the demarcations among anarchists are chronically unclear. That is why anarchist organising (even for those anarchists who do organise) can never adequately form a "memory of the working class" — never adequately and systematically work over the lessons of past struggles to bring ideas from them to new struggles.

Anarchism and a classless society: a reply to AWL

By North London Solidarity Federation

Solidarity 204, 18 May 2011

URL: bit.ly/kcy4RJ

Anarchism, as the author points out in "Working-Class Struggle and Anarchism", is a rather broad label, so it would be hopeless to try and identify a single tendency with all of its various groupings.
Similarly Marxism, historically and currently, has a million and one offshoots ranging from North Korea and Open Marxism to the SWP. Trying to refer to them all in blanket fashion as "Marxism" would be futile.

Many anarchists would see themselves as being broadly in the tradition of anarcho-syndicalism. The Solidarity Federation, for example, takes a lot of inspiration from the CNT in Spain among others, yet we do not see this as the be all and end all of struggle or a blueprint to follow. It is just a series of moments in time — nothing more nothing less. We can learn from its successes and failures like any other moment.

The idea promoted in the AWL's article seems to be the grand claim that anarchists "historically identify" with the peasantry. Now we could sit here all day and argue the ins and outs of class amongst the larger cash crop farms of the Ukraine and its smaller more subsistence-based ones a century ago, but I'm not really sure what relevance this has to Britain in 2011. Since thankfully none of us are Maoists, and hardly anyone is a peasant in Britain anymore, perhaps it's safe to say we can leave such debates to academia for now.

So for the purposes of this reply, We'll try to talk about anarchism as relevant to today in the UK. The goal of most anarchists is a stateless, wage-less, egalitarian, and industrial society. A society without money where, to borrow a phrase from Charlie M, production is based on human "need" and desire rather than "ability" to pay. This world, where money, war, class and poverty would be consigned to the history books has also been called communism and socialism. Though as with all words, being simply tools in the hands of their users, such terms have been used to describe societies and ideas that are very much the oppo-

99

site of their original meaning. In short anarchists want not "Taxation of the rich to fund decent public services...." as the "AWL, Labour and the Left" states, but the abolition of class relations altogether. In an anarchist society there will be no rich to tax and no money to collect.

The society we want to see should be mirrored by any movement or organisation that fights for it today. We want a society with direct democracy, a society in which we don't have politicians and/or representatives (elected or otherwise) telling us they will sort out our problems on our behalf. Thus, our movements and groups should be open and democratic, not relying on a leadership clique—whether that clique are parliamentary politicians or paid officials of a party or union.

A communist society would be one of workers' self-management, where we run our own workplaces and communities democratically and without bosses and wages. To get anywhere near this goal then, today we need movements based in our workplaces and communities. How could teachers and support staff collectively run a school or doctors, nurses and porters collectively run a hospital, unless we all had some experience of self-organisation, of acting on our own initiative rather than having bosses and politicians make all our decisions for us?

Deference to the Labour Party or to trade union leaderships will get us nowhere. If on the rare occasion we can strike and/or win within the current legal framework, then great, but seeing as generally we can't, we have to go beyond those limitations.

We need actions on the job and wildcats and occupations. These are the sorts of tactics that will get the goods where timid negotiations and one day symbolic strikes fail.

This may mean being inside or outside a mainstream union depending on the specifics of where you work [1]. The Solidarity Federation pushes for actions organised by everyone in a workplace, rather than along the narrow lines of demarcation placed by unions competing for members and/or 'professional respect'. In schools, for example, we would argue for meetings and actions that included all workers on site, in opposition to the way in which current union structures reinforce divisions between teachers and support staff.

We don't support the Labour Party. This isn't just because of its "historic role". It's because it looks a bit silly to be telling people you want both a socialist society and a Labour government. The two are entirely contradictory aims, and no amount of "fighting inside the Labour Party" can solve that. Certain union leaders such as McCluskey would have us believe that striking against Labour councils is somehow "awkward." Likewise, sections of the left portray the privatisation of NHS, and education cutbacks as being purely "Tory cuts" rather than an acceleration of previous Labour policies legitimised by a recession. Anarchists see no use in spreading such shallow sentiments.

Campaigns can't be won by waiting for a national leadership to sort your problems out for you. This means taking greater degrees of initiative, whether it's within union branches, within the anti-war movement. Surely we don't need reminding how the STWC's centralised approach stifled the anti-war movement in A-B marches and Respect recruitment drives. Similarly, in most UK workplaces, unions have no presence and even those that do are rarely "organised" in any real sense. In any case, workers need to be organising on the shopfloor to build the power, confidence, and skill of our class, not hoping to bring in union negotiators to speak on our behalf.

The North London Solidarity Federation would rather not get involved with debates over the historical minutiae of the past. In fact, they cloud real everyday issues. For example, the question of how local political or campaign groups should federate to a regional or national organisation and how a delegate council might make decisions based on mandates given by groups, as opposed to an elected or central and unelected committee is more important than the ins and outs of Bakunin and Marx's exchange of letters.

These questions about democracy and branch/group autonomy are not questions about abstract principles; they relate directly to how effective our fight back can be.

To conclude, anarchists are in full favour of healthy debate within the anti-capitalist movement. However, we believe these debates can only be productive if they are not inhibited by hierarchical structure that inevitable create a division between leaders and the led.

In short, "the emancipation of the working class must be the act of the workers themselves." It is this self-activity that will allow us to build a society based on our own desires, rather than having them handed down from above.

[1]. See the SolFed industrial strategy: bit.ly/twBqG1

We should work in the mass organisations: a reply to SolFed

By Stuart Jordan

Solidarity 205, 25 May 2011

URL: bit.ly / uJd2WU

SolFed's contribution to our debate on anarchism and class struggle (*Solidarity* 204) makes good use of the "straw man" technique of debate. This is arguably a bigger block on healthy debate in the anti-capitalist movement than the "inhibitions" caused by a "hierarchical structure"... whatever that means. Before we can explore the interesting points of difference, it is necessary to clear away some of the straw.

We are not for "taxation of the rich to fund public services" as an end goal. We are for a classless society based on the principle of "from each according to their ability to each according to their need". Our disagreement with SolFed is how to achieve that goal. (There is an interesting debate here about the use of transitional demands but it will have to wait for another day.)

No one in Workers' Liberty "defers to the Labour Party or to trade union leaderships". We do not believe that the trade unions should stay within the "limitations of the current anti-trade union laws". We think New Labour was a project of capitalist class war. We are in favour of striking against Labour governments and Labour councils (and we think workers should have the right to strike against any future socialist governments).

Our point of disagreement is about how we relate to mass working-class organisations.

SolFed aims to initiate "anarcho-syndicalist unions". Its members sometimes hold union cards "to avoid splits in the workplace between union members and non-union members". But their involvement in the unions is purely tactical and secondary to the main task of creating organisations apart from the actually existing trade union movement with its seven million members.

Workers' Liberty believes there is a class struggle taking place within

102

the mass organisations of the working-class and it is unrevolutionary to abandon those organisations to their middle-class leaderships. The trade union bureaucrats maintain power through a conscious effort to keep the workers docile, apolitical and hopeless. Our task is to fight for a working-class programme and the fullest possible participative democracy within the unions right now.

The struggle to build union strength against the bosses is also the struggle to organise workers against the bureaucracy. The process of creating revolutionary trade unions will involve many splits and fusions. It is very improbable that Unite, Unison and the Labour Party will be organising mass strikes and political action in the heart of a working-class revolution. But we cannot ignore these mass organisations of our class in 2011. The struggle to change them for the better is an experience our class needs in order to create political equipment for the future.

SolFed equate the bureaucratic structures of the trade union movement with the hierarchy of the "Leninist" party. But this is dishonest.

The mass, participative, democratic organisations that SolFed advocate would involve an organic leadership (elected individuals) linked to a base. That is a form of hierarchy.

The problem is not one of "hierarchy" as such but whether a leadership is accountable and uses its limited power to encourage democratic involvement and empower the rank-and-file.

The history of our class shows many revolutionaries — including syndicalists — who have won the leaderships of mass organisations in order to more effectively argue for their political ideals. They did not stand for election in order to win power for power's sake.

SolFed look at Stop the War Coalition, the trade union movement and the Labour Party and diagnose a problem of "hierarchy". We look at these organisations and diagnose a problem of "middle-class politics". True, politics cannot be divorced from questions of organisation, but SolFed stand the relationship on its head. In their scheme, the hierarchical form of organisation creates the middle-class politics. In fact, the bureaucratic structures are necessary to graft middle-class political leadership (be it the Blairites, the six-figure salaried trade union leaders, or the Muslim Association of Britain) onto a working-class base. Our task is to make clear these contradictions and build up rank-and-file organisation to challenge the leadership politically and organisationally.

At any given time, some people have a deeper understanding, more resolve, courage, experience or ability than others. If this were not the case, then revolutionary organisations would not need to exist.

Leaders in any context are only there to inspire others and help more effectively build our movement. We believe, like you, that the unions need to be built from the ground up. However, we differ from you in that we believe that a principled revolutionary leadership is necessary, possible and, importantly, can and should renew itself.

Workers' Liberty's idea of a revolutionary party is one which aims to group together the most politically class conscious workers to intervene in the movement against the political organisations of bourgeoisie and petit-bourgeoisie.

We do not believe that we are that revolutionary party but we organise in the spirit of the organisation we want to build in the future. Nor do not we think that this organisation is a model for a future society, any more than we think a workers' militia is a model for a classless society.

We do not equate hierarchy with bureaucratism but with experience tested in struggle. We want the maximum democracy and transparency.

The elected leadership of AWL is subject to constant scrutiny and can be recalled by the membership. We have freedom to form factions, open access to the press, and we are obliged to explain our differences with the majority line in public.

SolFed neglect to engage with the working-class movement as it really exists — with leaders (which are wholly inadequate) and hierarchy which is about bureaucracy. They construct an ideal working-class movement in their heads and try and call that ideal into being.

Yet through our approach — through engaging with the messy, compromised and often corrupted labour movement — we have been able to help organise the illegal direct action and rank-and-file organisation that you advocate. It was our initiative that has built one of the most successful rank-and-file organisations in the country on the London Underground. Our initiative was responsible for sparking the Vestas occupation of 2009.

If we were bigger, and more united with serious class-struggle organisations such as SolFed — even to a limited extent — then we would all be able to achieve much more.

Through joint work we would seek to convince you, through the process of struggle, to our revolutionary praxis of testing theory in the real arena of class struggle, the mass organisations of our class.

Climate Camp shuts down… itself

By Bob Sutton

Solidarity 196, 9 March 2011

URL: bit.ly / vJ94hW

The Camp for Climate Action, a network of direct-action environ-mentalists, whose main activity has been to organise a series of annual protest camps between 2006-2010, has dissolved itself. I was involved with the network for most of that time.

The 2007 Climate Camp at the site of the proposed third runway at Heathrow airport was the first political activity I got seriously involved in. I already thought of myself as a socialist and had read a couple of things. Growing up and going to school and college where I did had given me an embryonic understanding of class, and racism. But it was all half-baked.

The political baggage I had inherited from my parents, both one-time members of the Revolutionary Communist Group, meant that I thought the most useful thing for me to do was finish my A-levels, then head to Latin America and put myself at the disposal of either the Cuban or the Venezuelan regime. I'm quite lucky I didn't ever get very far.

It was through a friend from college that I found out about the camp. He had been part of the Forest School Camps, where a lot of the friend-ship groups that made up the core "cadre" of the Camp had originated.

The camp was not like anything I'd ever seen. 2,000 people in a squat-ted field in West London living, cooking, washing together. It seemed to be the closest thing to "communism" going on in that part of the world. I thought it was great. The process of endless meetings, run according to "consensus decision making" struck me as being massively wasteful and self-indulgent. The only thing I could counterpose it to in my head was a group of bearded guys in berets giving orders (in Spanish).

I had never planned on getting particularly involved, but I had noth-ing better to be doing and so stayed around. I was part of something which felt big, fresh, inspiring and youthful. It was showing how the world could be different, and pulling off some very impressive con-frontations with the police.

Through being part of one of these confrontations and some bad luck,

I was arrested and falsely charged with assaulting two police officers. This put the trip to Latin America on hold. But I stayed involved, largely getting into a lot of the practical skills stuff.

The 2008 camp was at the Kingsnorth coal fired-power station, where I threw myself into chopping wood and resisting the cops. It was here that I first really met members of the Alliance for Workers' Liberty. They were organising the Workers' Climate Action contingents that were leafleting the plant each morning, holding a meeting on women and the miners' strike. They got Clara Osagiede, leader of the London Underground cleaners' strike, to speak, got Arthur Scargill to come and debate on coal. They took the piss out of me for my Hugo Chavez t-shirt and a boycott Israel sticker, but they also wanted to know what I thought about the world.

They proposed a form of anti-capitalism which made sense to me, looking to the working-class, to solidarity, to challenge and overthrow the system and its horrors.

It increasingly became clear that most people involved in Climate Camp saw capitalism as something to pour a bucket of paint over. They conceived of the camp, and other "protest movements", as a ready-made utopia that would penetrate and spread over the old rotten order like a virus, and create a world in its image.

Moreover, when "off site" and faced with the real world and the questions it poses, the politics drawn upon were basically a variant of NGO left-liberalism. The underlying premise of a lot of the "direct action" is that "getting in the media" is the be all and end all — the bourgeois press is the only conceivable conduit of "revolutionary" politics.

I became increasingly aware of how this conception of "activists" as the agency for change in the world was a block to those people effectively making solidarity. Relatively few "campers" made it down to the Vestas wind turbine factory workers' occupation, while thousands descended on Blackheath in South London to camp "against the city", largely ignoring the working-class communities in the area.

I think the role of the Climate Camp was, following on from the "conference-hopping" protest movements of earlier in the decade, a way for middle-class anti-capitalists to generate confrontation with the state. It's a symptom of the low level of real class struggle. Therefore it was always characterised by a short attention span and a disregard for patient organisational or educational work.

Consensus is a form of organising shaped by these politics. It militates against scientifically thrashing out ideas, or any real notion of commitment to common struggle or accountability — no one is obliged to do anything they don't want to do.

There is much more to be said about the matter. I do hope however that the dissolution of the Camp will be part of a wider process of thrashing these questions out in the struggle to develop a coherent fight against the cuts.

The Anti-Cuts Movement and the Left

By the Anarchist Federation

Organise! 77, Winter 2011

URL: afed.org.uk/org/org77.pdf

The way to defeat the cuts, or to get close enough to rattle the State, is clear to the Anarchist Federation. It maps neatly onto our strategy for encouraging a "culture of resistance" in everything we are involved in.

This means struggle in many types of arena, and at different scales: neighbourhoods, cities, communities of identity, as recipients of welfare, in the workplace, and service user groups, for example. It means people fighting to defend their own interests but through this activity, realising that the state cannot provide for us; and if the State does make concessions, it does not do so because they are in our interests.

Through struggle and through analytical reflection on the futile process of beseeching the state, it becomes clear that we have to link up in a mass movement of generalised resistance. Resisting in the interests of our own cause alone only wins temporary gains that can be taken away again.

Common cause and mutual solidarity, if structured on a mass level, take us one step closer to a society that recognises that social revolution — the collective abolition of property and hierarchical social relations — will eliminate the need to have to struggle ever again.

The anti-cuts movement is an obvious example of a culture of resistance; it is where pockets of resistance meet, all the better because it is happening spontaneously. Once again the class is ahead of the propagandists!

Anarchists have to point out to the everyday heroes of the struggle that they are acting like anarchists, free from the constraints of reformism and representative democracy, practising direct action and direct democracy.

Except that mass resistance is being potentially ruined, once again, by the authoritarian Left! As usual, it is the Trotskyists who, having won influence within the struggle because of their numbers and resources, are now set to derail it.

As the Alliance for Workers' Liberty say on their website: "Our priority is to work in the workplaces and trade unions, supporting workers' struggles, producing workplace bulletins, helping organise rank-and-file groups".

But that's not where this struggle will be won. Workers' organisations of any sort are only part of the picture, and trade unions are legally castrated and effectively self-interested at that. We can't afford to let the Left divert the efforts of grass-roots activists into helping them win influence within the trade unions, which seems to be the latest turn in this experiment with working with the Left.

THE LEFT

We say "experiment", because it has been just that. The vast majority of anarchist activists wouldn't touch the authoritarian Left with a bargepole.

Many Left parties openly admit that on the eve of a "successful" revolution, they would have to eliminate anarchists! But that's not the real reason we don't enjoy working with most of them. It's because of their manipulative and deceitful attitude to the working class (it's difficult to come up with a better definition of the "Transitional Demand" than that). Also, it's because they fetishise the state to the extent that they willingly collaborate with it at the same time as "Fighting the Tories", or the EDL and BNP.

Lots of them fetishise the Labour Party too, being in it or hoping to get back in, to influence it from within (Alliance for Workers' Liberty), or building in parallel to it (Socialist Party), and much of their activity is in response to Labour rather than in response to class interests.

Then there is naked sectarianism, for example in the acrimony between the "Right to Work" campaign (Socialist Workers Party) and National Shop Stewards Network (Socialist Party).

Other problems include their propensity to duck in and out of struggles in ways that make it clear that they subordinate local struggles to national initiatives. This is alien to an anarchist way of thinking, in which national movements and initiatives are built from the base up.

And, at the end of the day, they run terrible meetings that exclude people not trained (often formally) to dominate the content of the discourse (reformism, substitutionism, obsession with the workplace, etc.) and the nature of that discourse (motions, amendments, formal hierarchy, informal deference shown to leaders, packing meetings and block votes, wilfully misrepresenting what other people say, and so on).

So why the experiment, when we can reliably predict the result? Firstly, because, except in major cities, it is very difficult to launch an anti-cuts campaign that will attract ordinary people to political activism unless it is at once big, dynamic, socially and culturally diverse, resourceful and welcoming.

Anarchists cannot provide this. Let's face it, we don't have the numbers, come from a narrower cultural background (a generalisation, but there's truth in it), and don't have the recent track record. We state our politics up front and sometimes that scares people. On the face of it, we aren't as attractive.

Second, because loads of members of Trotskyist organisations are hard-working, reliable, straightforward and personable. You can actually look forward to going for a drink with them after the meeting. They offer to help you with a task you've just taken on because, as usual, no one else offered at the time. They are entirely genuine about the struggle and are the hardest working in their party and union.

They have a sense of humour, skills to share, and get on with similarly non-sectarian members of other groups. They've never heard of Kronstadt; so you tell them, they look horrified, go away and read up on it, come back and say sorry (it's actually happened a few times!).

Most importantly, this struggle is simply too important to miss the opportunity of building a genuinely large, broad-based campaign. If we can't reverse the cuts, the working class is screwed. Even though we know that at some point things will probably turn sour with the Left, we know that it won't be us who proves impossible to work with; it will be the Trots. And the people who came to the campaign to be grassroots activists will remain as non-sectarian as they can, and will remain activists long after the Trots realise that they can't take the group by sheer force of numbers, belligerence, deceit and manipulation. Instead the Trots will leave the broad-based campaign in favour of struggle for power in the unions. We have to play a part in not letting them take over, as we did in the Poll Tax struggle (versus Militant, now Socialist Party), but failed in the Stop the War Coalition (versus Socialist Workers Party), for example.

There follows an interview with an Anarchist Federation member in Nottingham about the anti-cuts struggle there and the AF's experience of working in a genuinely broad-based campaign with the Left in it: Notts Save Our Services.

How did Notts SOS start, why were you involved, and why was it so immediately successful?

In October 2010 the Anarchist Federation nationally had decided against trying to set up either a national campaign or specifically anarchist-based campaigns in our towns.

Anarchism then didn't have the interest and respect that it has since gained. So Notts AF had been trying to get local people interested in a campaign against the cuts. We were doing our own thing, as were other anarchists in Nottingham, and often we were doing them together.

But it wasn't getting anywhere. Loads of people we spoke to thought it was great that someone was making a stand, but they didn't help us make an impact. I think people were too overwhelmed at the scale of what we faced. We almost managed to play a part in getting a claimants group set up, but I think we peaked too soon!

It was bad timing for us too, in that we had just set up the Sparrows' Nest and wanted to establish a focus for the serious study of Anarchism. We weren't going to neglect that. It just meant that we were working ourselves into the ground. But it would be worth it if we could help establish a broadbased campaign against the cuts locally.

So, when the Trades Council set up a public meeting, we went along to see if there were 'real' people there who we could work with. They were there in droves. We also went to slag off the Labour MPs they'd invited to speak. That went down very well indeed! In fact no one has ever spoken on behalf of the Labour Party at a Notts SOS meeting since, and it hasn't necessarily been us blocking it.

So, loads of people we'd never met before were wanting to get something going, and some of the people on the Trades Council who are nice as people and genuinely hard-working were there. Although we planned never to work formally in alliance with the Left again after the Poll Tax, we had done anti-BNP and EDL work with some of the Alliance for Workers' Liberty and Socialist Party and that had gone sort-of OK. And the Trades Council were going to kick start it with some cash for meeting rooms and leaflets. So, we got on board.

Within a few weeks, two-thirds of people at meetings — often of 40+ people, which is amazing for Nottingham — were people we'd never met before. From our first demo in November 2010, people joined SOS who have worked consistently hard and gone on to form Notts Uncut and a couple of initiatives around the NHS.

Those people also worked for threatened projects, e.g., housing support, and were teachers, retired people, jobcentre workers, activists on disability issues, etc. Lots of them have since lost their jobs but are still active protecting what remains.

Along with these sorts of people, we fought hard for a non-hierarchical structure for SOS, which it has retained very effectively.

The spin-off campaigns also organise non-hierarchically. This is really important. Setting up a structure with a Chair — people who will make statements and decisions for you — doesn't ever seem to have been considered by these groups, whereas 10 years ago that was the norm.

It's not non-hierarchical in quite the way anarchists mean it — sometimes it's more like a reflection of the structures of social media — but it's non-centralised and directly democratic, in that people don't speak or make decisions on other people's behalf without their permission.

Anyway, we've done some great stuff. There would have been no presence at the Labour-controlled City Council meeting that set the budget in April if not for SOS. We managed to stop the meeting and gave the council leader Jon Collins a really hard time.

We've also helped more local anti-cuts groups set up, and campaigns around libraries and to save Sherwood Forest. We set up the best anti-cuts website ever. OK, I'm biased, 'cos someone in the AF set it up and maintains it!

We use it to support and publicise campaigns such as ones to keep schools open and to preserve ESOL provision. We also helped link up the students in Nottingham Students Against Fees and Cuts with activists in the city. Staff and students at both universities work together all the time now.

The students inspired so much further activity. We helped them with a demo in support of EMA, and this brought even school and college students into the struggle. In fact that feels normal now, but then it was incredible: 16-year-olds chasing Collins all over the town centre, even though cuts to EMA weren't actually his fault.

They were so up for it! They made the connections: actually, he could have spoken up for students, but he didn't. Also, we ran a conference attended by over 70 people, out of which grew groups working on the NHS, benefits, education cuts and others that still exist. SOS supported fire stations, libraries, the list goes on. SO much work!

I was really proud to go on the London March 26th demo as a member of my profession alongside Notts SOS and workplace colleagues. Colleagues helped us carry our brilliant SOS banner, made by teachers in SOS. I chose attending the demo with these people over meeting up with the AF. And afterwards, SOS people defended the "black block" action, just as they had the Millbank students. I thought we might have to argue the toss over those events, but no one in Notts SOS had the slightest problem with what happened.

What went wrong?

We managed to ride out the first thing that nearly wrecked the campaign. It was a case of "what doesn't kill you makes you stronger". It was when we got into trouble with the Communication Workers' Union.

Notts SOS were running a modest stall every Saturday in the town centre. One Saturday, down the road there was going to be a big national CWU demo in support of their dispute. On the e-mail list someone pointed out that this would mean that we might be short on volunteers for the stall. The main guy in the CWU went ballistic that we weren't going to cancel our stall for their rally! This was even though the implication of the e-mail was that most people who usually volunteer would be at the rally instead.

The CWU guy took his complaint to the Trades Council. He was basically saying that SOS was being anti-union. The TC passed a motion supposedly unanimously (although we know that isn't true) making it clear that we had to toe the TC line or they'd stop bankrolling us.

This implied that they think social struggles should be subordinated to TU-controlled workplace struggles. We see the two as equally valuable in theory, and certainly the Left don't deny that the two are connected. But there is a whole world of difference between the 'workplace struggle' and 'the trade unions'. We have to be realistic; the days when the trades unions could make or break a government are gone. They don't control the Labour Party anymore. Capitalism has been far cleverer than the unions. Effective industrial action is now almost illegal, but the unions won't defy the law. So why should they be able to tell people engaged in direct action in social struggles what to do?

But SOS was on a roll by then and the campaign so broad-based that even though the AWL championed the TC motion and made sure it got accepted, everyone else decided to effectively ignore it.

We all thought it was a bit silly really. What was the worst that they could do in practice? The people who ran the stalls carried on doing stalls and supporting workers. We also started making collections for rooms and the NUT and NUM retired chapter started printing leaflets for us! So it wasn't the case that trade unionists as a whole felt threatened by our increasingly autonomous campaign.

Meanwhile other initiatives were springing up. Everyone knew how serious things were. Some anarchists in SOS wanted a specifically anarchist campaign, and others wouldn't touch SOS with a bargepole anyway. The result — Anarchists Against the Cuts — is small but has done creative stuff, made an intervention with propaganda, and brought some people out of the woodwork.

We've been involved since the beginning, even though its strategy doesn't make as much sense to us as being in an organisation that people can actually meet, work with and join if they agree with it.

We sometimes do the same theoretical groundwork twice, in AF and then in AATC, and feel a bit constrained by synthesis groups anyway. But there are spin-off campaigns where AATC, AF, SOS and Uncut, etc., overlap, and Left and nonaligned people know that the anarchist movement in Nottingham isn't just AF (which it certainly isn't).

One of the best local victories was anarchist-inspired. It prevented the cutting of outpatient services at Hayward House, a hospice. The campaign sprung up overnight and mobilised terminally ill people, which scared the shit out of the Primary Care Trust.

It went for the jugular on financial, ethical and legal grounds, and forced the trust to back off and even admit that it had made a mistake. It took a massive amount of work over a very short time and won by being a full-on, uncompromising onslaught of common sense! But victory had not a little to do with the fact that the people initiating the campaign — volunteers and fundraisers for the hospice — were also long-standing anarchist activists who know how to win. This all happened before SOS had even undertaken any support work! So there is evidence that anarchists don't necessarily fight the cuts best as part of SOS.

Is that why you are despondent about the broad-based campaign?

In part. But it's also because we've entered another phase in which the Trotskyists have regrouped and decided they haven't been focussing on the workplace enough. I was on a sort of ad-hoc committee that was organising the Nottingham events on June 30th. Representatives of the three striking unions were part of it: NUT, UCU and PCS, and other people supporting us, notably Nottingham Students Against Fees and Cuts (although they quickly realised that they were being patronised and could support the strike better in other ways).

At the end of the day, when it comes to the crunch, trade union activists have to be more concerned with their members' sectional interests than in wider struggle. NUT members weren't very interested on the whole in anything other than their pensions (I'm not saying that's not important; we are rightly supportive of workers with good terms and conditions maintaining them as a way to encourage less privileged workers to make a stand for their own rights). Their officers include AWL members, who are politically miles ahead of those narrow sectional interests. The officers agreed to a demo that would march past places like the homeless shelter, NHS Direct, ATOS, Office Angels and the banks.

Then the NUT officers started messing us around and changing the arrangements, because when they'd gone back to their members they'd had a right telling off!

They'd made decisions for their members — see what I mean? They had to come back and tell us that no, they were going to have the usual A-B march and then have an indoor rally. The biggest demo Nottingham had seen for years, and they wanted to take it indoors to discuss NUT pensions!

The NUT also started making up stuff about the police and council being obstructive about logistics for an outdoor rally, which wasn't true. The UCU and PCS activists were furious. One meeting got so acrimonious that the chair had to intervene at one point and tell a particularly belligerent person to "take it outside!"

The official and unofficial representatives of both UCU and PCS crossed over massively with SOS, Notts Uncut, NSAFC, and were completely in agreement with the idea of making the march and rally an 'in-your-face-Cameron' protest about the cuts generally. Given that it was on a weekday too, so places were open, this could actually have terrified ATOS out of business! I really think so.

We had some good stuff planned. Instead, the only aspect of social struggles that got a look in at the rally was SOS and the NHS campaign. We were allowed to speak on the platform, but last, when almost everyone had gone home.

We haven't really recovered from that demo. We worked so hard as SOS to support the striking unions, but I don't think either we or the PCS and UCU will work with the NUT again. And the AWL came out of it looking like opportunists.

To be honest, I think we also lost credibility as anarchists. I wasn't able to argue our corner, and I was there informally representing our workplace campaign group. To be honest, I felt too intimidated to say anything much.

Straight after, it was the Bombardier stuff. All the Left groups wanted us to drop everything and pile over to Derby, there even before we'd established that this wasn't going to be some nationalistic German-bashing thing (which it wasn't). We actually had a really good discussion and I was impressed by the unforced internationalism of all three Left groups.

But again, they wanted influence in there. I think they wanted to take Notts SOS over to Derby to get kudos. We couldn't go anyway, but we'd have gone as anarchists, not in some Trot rent-a-demo.

And at the same time, every meeting started getting TU focussed again, discussing how bad the internal politics of, for example, Unison are, and how we need to get socialists elected within them. Don't get me wrong, there are Notts SOS activists I'd far rather have represent me or have influence within my union than some New-Labourite. In particular, there are several people in Unison in Nottingham and Notts who are in or around Left parties who are genuinely great people. But at the end of the day everyone (else) knows that the Left's struggles for control of the unions mean nothing at all to the rest of the working class, who either can't unionise or don't see the point.

I would say to any of them, you should join a union to protect your interests, and if there's anyone in your workplace up for a fight, that's where you'll meet them. But if they asked where the potential for class struggle really is now, I'd point them in other directions.

So is that it for Notts SOS, as far as you are concerned?

Not at all. There's still loads of potential. There is a tendency at the moment for non-aligned people or people in political minorities to be despondent, and several have effectively and even officially left the campaign.

But I don't think there's been a time when anarchist ideas have had more influence. It no longer feels utopian to call for occupations, mass assemblies, blockades, sabotage, non-compliance, etc. People in Nottingham are not afraid of these things. I was amazed how much support the students had last year, for example. Notts SOS had people in it very new to political action and they thought the student riots and occupations were brilliant. Notts Uncut shuts down 3 or 4 businesses of a Saturday and gets a really good crowd. People stand and listen to them. The NHS campaign occupied a huge roundabout in town for hours (it also hung a life-size effigy of Andrew Lansley, which was a bit controversial!).

I think Notts SOS should be a hub and a support for these and even more daring sorts of direct action. In itself, it can't be radical because it can't seem to do anything public without informing the police and

Labour City Council at some point.

That's because the Left still have this split personality where they both critique and fetishise the Labour Party at the same time, insisting that its membership is better than its leadership. That's only a meaningful analysis if the membership can control the leadership, which it can't. That's what happens when you elect people to make decisions on your behalf!

Some of the Left activists actually stood as Labour councillors and got in, and we haven't seen them since at SOS; inevitably, because they are now representatives of a party that is pro-cuts!

At the end of the day, when you look at the website — which you should — we haven't actually done our most impressive work as SOS. Rather, it's been the groups SOS has spawned, fostered and championed. We bring these together in one place in a way that no other organisation possibly can. But at the end of the day, SOS is a little too timid. It's clear that even though people will say they support the idea of, say, a student-led occupation of a city centre building, they might wander along, but they won't commit to anything that might marginalise workplace-focused activism. They don't really get it. So SOS should continue, but either try to free itself from this inertia or maintain its role as a focal point.

It can't go down the reformist route and be beholden to the trades unions. Members of the Left organisations have a choice. They have to ask themselves where their priorities lie and be honest about it.

Anarchism, the anti-cuts movement, and working-class politics

By Tom Unterrainer

Abridged / edited from an article on the AWL website, 6 May 2012

URL: bit.ly / MkGzKj

The Winter 2011 issue of the Anarchist Federation's (AFed) magazine *Organise!* carries a long article detailing some of the history of the Nottinghamshire Save Our Services campaign.

As well as providing a sometimes valuable narrative of events, AFed take the opportunity to attack their political opponents in the campaign. The main focuses for their ire are "the Trotskyists" and the Alliance for Workers' Liberty in particular. Throughout the article, these groups are referred to as "the Left".

Of course, AFed have every right to print and publish what they like — even attacks on the AWL. We warmly welcome the opportunity to respond and to continue the debates we initiated with anarchist comrades in 2011. But before we respond to specific points, some general comments about the structure of the article and AFed in Nottingham are necessary.

STARTING ARGUMENTS WHEN WE NEED DEBATE

The article — "The Anti-Cuts Movement and the Left: A local activist's perspective" — is not an interview with any old local activist as its title and Q&A style suggests.

In fact, the person being interviewed is probably a long-standing anarchist activist in Nottingham and, it is safe to assume, a prominent member of AFed. The folksy language used throughout aims to charm, but it cannot mask the fact that this is a factional, politically focussed attack.

Throughout the article, the interviewee states or implies that one of the problems with the "Left" is that they claim to represent or speak for large constituencies of people (members of a trade union branch, the working class as a whole, etc.) when in fact they speak only for themselves.

The article finds the "Left" guilty as charged, but in doing so reproduces exactly the attitudes AFed claims to reject. The comrades claim that one of their major tasks is to convince "the everyday heroes of the struggle that they are acting like anarchists" — and recruit them to AFed, we assume. The interviewee sets themselves up as not only the voice of the ordinary person involved in Notts SOS but the arbiter of who is and who is not a "nice", "hard-working" individual; who has a "sense of humour, skills to share", etc.

Whilst AFed claim to be non-hierarchical, they are not shy in imposing a hierarchical set of measures to assess who and who is not a worthwhile participant in the struggle.

The article suggests that whilst poor little AFed is fighting to stop other groups from dominating Notts SOS, the massed forces of the Nottingham "Left", with their "greater numbers and resources", threaten to consume the campaign!

This is nonsense, especially when considered against the reality of the balance of forces on the ground. For instance, it's likely that AFed has more members in Nottingham than either the AWL or the SWP. Second, Nottingham AFed can boast an asset called the Sparrows' Nest — an anarchist study and resource centre. No group on the Nottingham "Left" has such facilities. So far from being a beleaguered, small and resource-less group of people fighting the good fight against nasty Trotskyists, Nottingham AFed are in fact blessed in comparison to the rest of us!

One last point on the political method of this article. Take this quote from early on as an example: "Many Left parties openly admit that on the eve of a 'successful' revolution, they would have to eliminate anarchists!"

My first question is: *who* "admits" such a thing? Specifically, which organisations with representatives in Nottingham make this claim? Are we to suppose that AFed comrades willingly sit around the table with people they assume to be their future executioners? If they do, then they are a special kind of masochist! It's not enough for AFed to paint the "Left" and Workers' Liberty members as "authoritarian" with a "deceitful attitude to the working class", no … we're future murderers to boot! This is not a serious political method. It's not the sort of method that encourages honest and open debate over differences of theory and tactics. It's playground stuff: a lesson in how to start a fruitless argument when what we should be having is a debate.

What follows is an attempt to critique some of the ideas expressed in AFed's article and address some of their specific criticisms. We hope it starts a useful dialogue.

"The anti-cuts movement is an obvious example of a culture of re-sistance; it is where pockets of resistance meet, all the better be-cause it is happening spontaneously."

The term "culture of resistance" is a regular feature of AFed literature — but what does it mean? The article itself doesn't explain, but the AFed publication *The Role of Revolutionary Organisation* states under the sub-heading "Culture of resistance" that: "[o]ur true sense of community and culture only comes to life when we resist, when our class acts for it-self ... Building links is an important task, links between cause and ef-fect, between struggles and campaigns, between ideas and theories, between people ... Don't try to force your ideas onto people as you will either split the group, exclude yourself or create de-energised and bored people, alienated from the idea and practice of revolution. Don't be rigid or push forward rigid formulas. People's views change through strug-gle, not by being harangued or having deadly theory shoved down their throats."

So the term not only refers to a set of conditions that others on the left would describe as class struggle, but to an attitude and way of behav-iour appropriate for "libertarian revolutionaries".

In *Beyond Resistance* (AFed's manifesto), the comrades use a clearer definition. In section C, sub-section 1 — "Pre-revolutionary Culture" — they write: "By this Culture of Resistance we mean the development of both social spaces and general attitudes of anti-capitalist combativity."

There is an undeniable element of spontaneity in the anti-cuts move-ment, as there is in any developing arena of struggle. Individuals and groups with whom we — revolutionaries — have no contact whatsoever will start to resist and take action when faced with a worsening of condi-tions or a sharp change of events. One thing that feeds our hopes for and understanding of the possibilities for revolutionary change is that when faced with adversity, human beings can and do resist of their own voli-tion.

But this understanding is only the beginning of wisdom. Humans, and the working class more specifically, do not enter the arena of struggle as blank slates. History, experience, culture and belief — the social relations between individuals, groups and society as a whole — shape the course of any action taken. Whatever the merits of humanity, we are not born with "good sense" hard-wired into our brains. We often adopt a "com-mon sense" approach formed and informed by limited experience and more or less irresistible influence ... irresistible if left uncontested, that is.

The Italian Marxist Antonio Gramsci put it this way: "Each individual is the synthesis not only of existing relations but also the history of these relations, the sum of all of the past". In a society shaped and formed by class struggle, but a society nonetheless based on exploitation and oppression — with the additional experience of multiple defeats for our class — "the history of these relations" weighs heavily upon us.

Taken literally, AFed's injunction against sharp argument would mean stepping back from sharp disputes with activists who argue for nationalistic, chauvinistic, racist or sexist positions. We know from practice that anarchists in general and AFed in particular are consistent and open critics of such thinking. Or is it acceptable to argue sharply against these ideas but not others we oppose — such as reformism and Stalinism?

The records of struggle show that reactionary ideas can be dispelled — or at least have the edges taken off — through struggle. For instance, the miners' strike of the 1980s and the solidarity shown by women and gays — to name but two groups — decisively shifted the world view of some strikers.

Can the same be said for ideas such as reformism and Stalinism? The record here shows that whilst small numbers of people can be compelled to reject such ideas through experience alone, the great bulk of evidence suggests that experience alone cannot shift large layers of society away from these views. Even the tumultuous collapse of "official" Stalinist communism in Russia and Eastern Europe failed to crush illusions in Stalinist ideas. The Communist Party may have withered, but the ideas endure in general political culture.

The experience of the Labour Party in government is another case in point. How much more vile than Tony Blair would a Labour prime minister have to be before "real-world experience" finally stopped people from voting Labour?

The fact is that many Stalinist ideas remain generally accepted — are "common sense" — even by those who have never been organised Stalinists. The same is true for passive hope invested in reformism through a vote for Labour. In short, some — but not all — bad ideas melt away through struggle. Indeed, struggle can generate a great deal of "common sense" to the detriment of "good sense".

Take, for example, the movement of the "outraged" (*indignados*) in Spain. A mass movement of the young, unemployed and underemployed, the *indignados* firmly rejected the Spanish government's plans to reform the labour market and benefits system. Both major parties — the social democrats who were in government at the time and the opposition conservative People's Party — supported the terrible legislation. In the face of a crisis ridden economy, other smaller opposition parties, to the left and right, stood ineffectually by. The trade union leaders initially voiced their opposition to the plans but only a minority called action in response.

Against this background, the spokespeople for the *indignados* professed their rejection of not only all political parties but also the unions. The rejection was total: meaning a total rejection of the political party and trade union forms of organisation. The "good sense" of the movement was a sharp critique of existing political structures and a rejection of their leadership — such a realisation has true revolutionary potential. The "common sense" that prevailed dispersed the revolutionary potential that an organised fight within the unions and the formation of new a party organisation could have maintained.

What happened? The biggest single thing that happened as a consequence of the Spanish crisis was the returning to power of the People's Party with a firm mandate to carry through biting austerity measures — something the social democrats lacked due to the level of opposition. Uncontested in the electoral arena and faced with an amorphous anti-political movement, the forces of neoliberalism got what they wanted. *The anti-political, "culture of resistance" failed the test of reality.*

The specific errors — or over-assumptions, if you like — and contradictions in AFed's definition of a "culture of resistance" can be summarised as follows:

First, the over-assumption: "People's views change through struggle, not by being harangued or having deadly theory shoved down their throats."

It is indeed true that ideas change through struggle — as they do when any altering of relations and conditions takes place. For instance, you touch a red-hot poker for the first time and you learn two things, (1) pokers that glow red are hot and (2) it's a very bad idea to touch a red-hot poker.

But you don't have to touch the poker to know it's a bad idea. One thing that separates humans from other animals is our ability to learn in the abstract — we can be told and understand it's a good idea not to touch things that are glowing red, for instance.

AFed are making an argument against arguing: that everything will come out right in the end because the struggle will sort any "bad" ideas out: "if only everyone realised they were acting like anarchists!" History tells us otherwise, does it not? Certainly the fate of the anarchist movement during the Spanish revolution and counter-revolution of the 1920s clearly demonstrates that terrible mistakes are possible even by anarchists faced with a revolution in the making.

The contradiction: is it the case that when the "Left" fights for its politics we "harangue" and "shove it down people's throats", whilst when AFed presents and defends its politics it does so in a soft and cosy fashion?

If it's the first, then what's the point in having a revolutionary organisation such as AFed where being the "memory of the class" and "revolutionary propagandists" is so highly prioritised? If people join the organisation, are all the facts revealed but they must promise to keep it to themselves? Is AFed in fact a secretive cult? Their website, plethora of pamphlets and publications suggests otherwise.

If it's the second, we have already described the realities and actual method AFed employs to defend its politics in the first section of this response. It may be of a more subtle variety, but the "harangue" is unmistakeable.

AFed's "culture of resistance" is a nice phrase but it appears to have a limited material basis. It's a "thing" that the AFed comrades are forever looking out for and can never quite find in acceptable form.

The weekly meetings of Notts SOS and the activities and demonstrations it organised were and are far removed from the high-pitch nature of other events around the world ... but according to AFed they are a "culture of resistance" nonetheless. Was this ever the case?

If you reject the all-or-nothing romanticism implied by AFed's phrase-making and settle for an examination of concrete reality, the results are less than spectacular but of huge potential significance.

The forces that initiated and combined into Notts SOS were impelled by the actual need to fight into an association of basic working-class solidarity. Significantly, this association brought together trade union activists, socialists, community campaigners and, yes, anarchists, to fight for a common but limited purpose. Notts SOS, like other anti-cuts groups around the country, represents the molecular processes of a potentially large-scale re-composition of the forces of struggle: the re-building of working class self-organisation and the fight for solidarity.

It's in this sense that Notts SOS has disappointed them, because having imagined that an anti-cuts "movement" would develop in a certain way and open certain opportunities for anarchist organisation, it did not bear fruit.

There is no direct correlation between general economic slump, political depression and a rejection of established political institutions on the one hand and an upturn in struggle on the other. To a certain extent, the grind of austerity economics has become a normal feature of everyday life. That this has happened is in no small part a consequence of the failures of trade union leaders — especially with regard to the pensions campaign — and the organised left. The evident impotence of the labour movement leaders and the lack of (for the most part — the Sparks dispute and moves currently under way in the National Union of Teachers being exceptions) rank-and-file pressure within the unions has fed into the downturn in anti-cuts work.

The fact that Nottingham AFed comrades cannot fully understand why, and draw general negative conclusions from their experience, is just one symbol of their political limitations.

THE AWL, TRADE UNIONS, AND THE ANTI-CUTS MOVEMENT
"...mass resistance is being potentially ruined, once again, by the authoritarian Left!"

Unable to conceive just why so many people failed to jump to anarchist conclusions or realise that they're really anarchists, AFed has to find someone to blame. It goes without saying that they're innocent on all matters (guilty only of having "lost credibility" because of too close an association with AWL "opportunists"!). The AWL on the other hand — and Nottingham comrades in particular — are dripping with blame from every pore.

"As usual, it is the Trotskyists who, having won influence within the struggle because of their numbers and resources, are now set to derail it" claim AFed. We have already dealt with the issue of "numbers and resources" in the introduction. But do not fear: the comrades have found a quote on the AWL website that justifies their claims. In fact, they didn't have to look very far to find this damning evidence because the quote they use is carried in every paper we print. The quote: "Our priority is to work in the workplaces and trade unions, supporting workers' struggles...", etc.

AFed warn: "[T]hat's not where this struggle will be won ... We can't afford to let the Left divert the efforts of grass-roots activists into helping them win influence within trade unions..."

Had the comrades dug a little deeper into our website — or simply typed "anti-cuts" into the search facility — they would have found our 2010 conference document "Trades councils and anti-cuts committees", where we agreed that:

"Whatever their exact nature or origin, the emergence of these [anti-cuts] committees and their future work is a key indicator of the future shape of resistance to the cuts. Such committees will attract layers of trade union and working class activists from a wide and rich layer of the movement, they represent a chance to rejuvenate and renew the labour movement in terms of personnel, ideas and initiative.

"We should note the immediate possibility and potential dangers of sections of the existing left attempting to 'coordinate' the work of these committees by engineering affiliations to their own front organisations. This is already the case with the SWP's Right to Work campaign and we should expect the Socialist Party to operate on their 'successful model' forged during the Poll Tax rebellion.

"We should encourage the involvement of Labour Party representatives in anti-cuts campaigns, but should not trim our activities, or limit our criticisms of Labour in order to keep them on board. We should use any such involvement to pressure Labour to adequately resist the Government."

It's likely that AFed comrades would find much to criticise in this selection and from the document as a whole, but rather than address our actual ideas they selected a small section from our basic statement "What is the Alliance for Workers' Liberty?" to indict us.

WHAT IS THE AFED SO HOTILE TO?

"But [the labour movement] is not where this struggle will be won" they write.

Further, "Workers' organisations of any sort are only part of the picture, and trade unions are legally castrated and effectively self-interested at that. We can't afford to let the Left divert the efforts of grass-roots activists into helping them win influence within the trade unions, which seems to be the latest turn in this experiment with working with the Left."

The comrades present themselves as hostile to the existing, mass trade unions and the broader labour movement. Unable or unwilling to address themselves to the realities of class struggle and the monumental history of our class which conditions the reality we face today, they cook up a conspiracy.

A more detailed account of AFed's attitude to the unions can be found in their pamphlet *On the frontline: anarchists at work*. This document — "Workplace Strategy of the Anarchist Federation" — summarises their views as follows:

"[The] contradiction between the union's role in disciplining and controlling workers and the material advantages and opportunities to organise that it brings cannot be wished away. Any militant in the workplace must find ways of working around these problems and find ways of using the opportunities and protections unions offer without being co-opted and controlled by union structures."

As you'd expect from a publication devoted to workplace strategy, the comrades present a more worked-out point of view than the selection above indicates. But the essence of their politics remains the same as that expressed by their actual political practice.

The AFed comrades are happy to accept the unions as a fact and embrace the "security" provided by the unions. All the same, militants must find a way around the problems posed by the union bureaucracy. This sort of attitude is antithetical to socialists for two reasons.

First, the conception of "union-as-safety-net" is shared by most trade union leaders and bureaucrats. Neither the union bosses nor militant anarchists — or more precisely the anarchist-communists of AFed — imagine the unions actually staging a fight or doing anything other than providing legal advice. For AFed, trade unionism is synonymous with workplace lawyerism.

Second, "finding a way around" the bureaucracy is something that neither "classical" anarchists nor socialists would be content with. Our aim is to smash the bureaucracy and to replace it with real, living and breathing democratic structures. Simply "finding a way around" rather than taking the bureaucracy on, challenging their leadership, standing in elections against them, etc., is abandoning an aspect of class struggle within organisations fought for and built by the working class. It's an abandonment of our history as a class and a rejection of the idea that mass organisations of workers can and do fight.

But AFed don't "abandon struggle" altogether do they? No, they have an answer; but the answer is sectarian to the core. Whilst relying on existing trade unions for legal advice, representation and protection (despite the fact that AFed considers trade unions to be nothing more than "mediating structures within capitalism"), the comrades advocate a strategy of building a "workplace resistance group" outside of and independent from the trade unions. Who is going to build and join these "resistance groups"? One can only suppose that AFed members will play a central role.

Unhappy with the trade unions — not only as they currently exist, but because they are nothing more than capitalist "mediating structures" — AFed wants to build its own workers' organisations separate from and uninterested in the majority of the organised working class. This is the quintessence of political sectarianism.

The "workplace resistance group" is not the be-all of their strategy for the working class. Far from it. The comrades advocate the idea of a "mass workers' assembly": "History has shown us repeatedly that the direct form which is the natural expression of working class political power is the mass assembly, and from this the use of mandated re-callable delegates to form the councils of workers required to oversee first revolutionary struggle, then the everyday functioning of the new society. Therefore, the mass workers' assembly is precisely the organisa-tional form we agitate for in order for the principles of self-organisation, direct action and mutual aid to become the leading ones within mass struggle. It is the expression of the anarchist communist goal..." [*On the frontline*]

Whereas AFed's propaganda for resistance groups jars with reality (for example, I'm not aware that any such groups exist where AFed mem-bers work in Nottingham), their call for a "mass workers' assembly" di-rectly contradicts what AFed members have said and done in Nottingham.

In the run-up to the 30 June 2011 pensions strike, members of AFed ar-gued against proposals from the National Union of Teachers locally (where two AWL members are active) to hold a strike meeting at the end of a demonstration. The NUT and AWL comrades were clear that this was to consist of a small number of speeches to be followed by a wide-ranging discussion on the future of the dispute. AWL members pointed out that only one day of action had been called so far and that to win on pensions we would need a serious campaign of industrial action. The AWL also attempted to explain that 30 June should be used to help or-ganise or re-organise (in some cases) trade union branches; that mem-bers of all unions need to come together to discuss and decide what action should be taken; and that we needed local organisation to put de-mands on the leaders of unions for further and consistently effective in-dustrial action.

AFed members from UCU opposed this suggestion and instead sup-ported calls from the Socialist Workers Party for a "Day of Rage" against the government. Whilst the "day of rage" failed to appear, the disrup-tion and disorientation produced by much quarrelling and back-biting reduced the strike meeting to nothing more than a rally. So much for the rhetoric of "mass workers' assemblies"!

LABOUR PARTY

"Some of the left activists actually stood as Labour councillors and got in, and we haven't seen them since at SOS; inevitably because they are now representatives of a party that is pro-cuts!"

As far as AFed are concerned, there seems to be only one organisation worse than Trotskyist groups or trade unions: the Labour Party.

They are so obsessed and so far from any rational understanding of either the Labour Party or the AWL's attitude towards it, that members of AFed come across as something akin to Third Period Stalinists in their fixated denunciations of all things "Labour". This fixation goes to the point of wilfully misrepresenting reality, as with the quote that opens this section.

The AFed comrade really wants it both ways on this score. At the same time as praising the flowering of anti-cuts and service user groups that emerged either independently from or inspired by Notts SOS, they can't bring themselves to praise the work done by two Labour Party councillors who had previously been central to getting SOS off the ground.

So what have these Labour councillors done since being elected? First, they organised a campaign to save a local library, which included a mass read-in attended by scores of local residents. Second, one of the councillors helped set up and run a local anti-academy campaign that has now grown into a county-wide "Hands Off Our Schools" group. Third, they waged a battle within the Labour Party for a vote against the upcoming cuts budget. They spoke in the council chamber against the cuts and voted against them — bringing another Labour Party councillor along with them. Finally, one of these Labour councillors who "we haven't seen since" continues to be the treasurer of Notts SOS — organising the finances, looking for donations, etc. It's likely that the AFed writer has had recent communications with this Labour councillor about room collection money!

So much for the idea that they've disappeared "because they are now representatives of a party that is pro-cuts!" Where reality doesn't fit their dogma, this AFed writer chooses distortion and half-truths.

So what is AFed's attitude to the Labour Party all about? Writing of Bakunin's relationship with the First International, Hal Draper notes: "Bakunin's was the first leftist movement to apply its conspiratorial pattern of subversion not to assail society at large or to defend itself against the police, but to destroy other socialists' organisation. Its rationale was

128

its own theory that these rivals were part and parcel of the Authoritarian Enemy, or maybe worse (compare the similar rationale, sixty-five years later, of the Stalinised Communist International with the adoption of the theory of social-fascism)."

["Bakunin and the International: A 'Libertarian' Fable", from *Karl Marx's Theory of Revolution, Volume IV: Critique of other socialisms*]

There are a number of problems with AFed's attitude. First — and paradoxically for anarchists — they seem unable to differentiate between members of the Labour Party and the leaders of the party. Second, they either have no understanding of or wilfully refuse to understand the organic connections and historical basis of the relationship between the Labour Party and the trade unions — however distorted and neutered these connections and relationships currently are. Third, because they essentially dismiss struggles within the trade unions for more effective action, more democracy and more accountable leadership they also fail to recognise the potential political ramifications of these fights on the Labour Party. Fourth, they assume that anyone on the left who maintains even a passing interest in what happens in the Labour Party somehow agrees with or is prepared to toe-the-line in fear of the party leadership. Fifth, they refuse to recognise or accept the realities of current struggles within the Labour Party — even when they are on their doorstep and within the bounds of their political contacts.

For AFed, Labour is no different from Tory. No historical considerations, no current facts and no amount of patient explanation seem to be able to shift them.

So rabid is their attitude against the Labour Party that they choose not to hear criticisms of Labour from those they assume to be mortally corrupted (e.g., AWL comrades). Further, they treat middle-of-the-road, not-very-left-wing, spineless and uninspiring Labour MPs as if they were fascists, by attempting to "no-platform" the Blairite MP Alan Meale after the Trades Council invited him (wrongly, but democratically) to address its 2012 May Day rally.

CONCLUSION

The events of May Day 2012 also add something to the overall picture of AFed's politics missing so far: their anti-democratic and consequentially authoritarian individualistic and moralistic outlook.

For those people attracted to anarchist ideas and principles, we say: "just look at what becomes of them". Whilst AFed is not representative of anarchism per se — indeed it's no more than one sect within the anar-

chist scene, a sect with which many anarchists want no association —
there are qualities within AFed common to anarchists of all outlooks.

Marxists and anarchists have a shared history: one littered with errors,
scandals, accusations, counter-accusations, controversy, and debate.
Marxists also have something in common with class-struggle anarchists:
an unmoveable hostility to capitalism and an understanding that we
need to organise for working-class revolution.

A dialogue and some level of understanding between Marxists and anarchists is desirable and potentially useful — as activists, we are involved in many common struggles within and without the workplace.

**But dialogue and debate can only usefully take place if it is on
terrain where neither party engages in distortion, misrepresenta-
tion, and deliberate avoidance of certain facts. The AFed's journal
article, and their Stalinist antics at May 2012, are typical of the kind
of attitude and actions that make fruitful dialogue and collaboration
much more difficult.**

Five things Trotskyists should know about today's young "anarchists"

By Yves Coleman

Yves Coleman is a French revolutionary who helps publish the journal *Ni patrie ni frontières* (mondialisme.org). This is an extended version of an address he gave at the AWL's 2011 conference on 22 October in which he criticised our recent polemics against anarchism. A version of the address was published in *Solidarity* 224, 9 November 2011.

URL: bit.ly/uFlSAR

"When I cook for the Occupy movement in London, I contribute to changing the world. " (An interviewee on RFI Radio)

As far as I know, the AWL is the only organisation in the European far-left which is trying to seriously debate with other reformist or revolutionary currents.

I don't share the AWL's dogmatic reverence toward Leninism and Trotskyism, but we have something important in common: the belief that discussions can be useful and fruitful as long as they are not led along sectarian and slanderous lines. I acknowledge your effort to deal with other currents of thought, even when I disagree totally with you.

Anarchist comrades should remember the virtues of political debates, particularly as Emma Goldman and Voltairine de Cleyre — to quote only two famous examples — participated in debates with socialists (Marxists) and were won over to anarchism through such debates!

So the question of debate is not where our disagreement regarding today's "anarchism" lies. It seems to me that your articles in *Solidarity* were too much centred on "old-style"19th-century anarchism and not on today's diverse, confused, libertarian and anarchist currents.

Through my work publishing the journal Ni patrie ni frontières (which, for almost 10 years, has published many anarchist and Marxist texts together in the same issue and on the same theme to stimulate debate and political reflection), I have had the occasion of meeting many young "anarchists" in book fairs, conferences, etc. What struck me is how much (generally) they ignore "their" classics: Proudhon, Bakunin,

131

Stirner or Kropotkin. There are certainly many more points to be discussed, but I would like in this article to underline only five.

TRAINING

When Trotskyists discuss with young "anarchists", they should realise that they did not receive, and don't value, the same "training".

Trotskyists are generally trained in "party" "schools" where they learn about the history of the workers' movement and the basic laws of Marxist "science". That was the tradition until the 70s and 80s in France in Trotskyist groups. In general the Trotskyist press still puts the stress on the importance of a historical culture. That has also happened in the Spanish CNT before World War II, or in some traditional anarchist groups before the 1960s, but is no longer true as far as I know in Europe.

Young European "anarchists'" political culture is much more diverse : it derives from all sorts of radical or marginal films or documentaries, semi-political zines and music, from the anti-globalisation movement and from all sorts of tiny booklets reproduced in "infokiosks", etc.

I must also say that for those anarchists with a solid background in revolutionary history, there is absolutely no forgetting (nor is there is the slightest wish to minimise) the deeds and thoughts of the historical figure known as Leon Trotsky. You are not going to persuade these anarchists about anything concerning Kronstadt 1921 or Nestor Makhno, because the role of Trotsky in suppressing these revolutionary movements is both well known and well documented. The Trotskyists' lies, slanders, and distortions about these historical episodes mean that anarchists with a grasp of the historical record will be immune to your overtures, and with good reason. They see classical Trotskyism as part of the problem, and in no way part of the solution.

DIRECT ACTION NOW

Trotskyists should realise that young "anarchists" today want action now. And by "action now" they don't mean a long "primitive accumulation" of militants (or cadres) to build the party (a process traditional Trotskyists enjoy so much).

The most "physical" (and sometimes "macho") anarchists want to confront physically the cops, to throw Molotov cocktails, to smash the face of fascists, to destroy the headquarters of some bourgeois party, etc. The more "peaceful" ones (but sometimes people who are also in the first group) want to build new human relationships here and now. That means organising squats or communes; questioning gender relationships now and not in a distant future under communism; cultivating vegetables to have healthy food; "skipping" good food from supermarket dustbins to distribute it or cook it; cooking food for homeless or poor people; supporting illegal workers' struggles concretely; occupying unemployment agencies; organising unemployed or precarious workers; creating cooperatives; discussing all sorts of ways of changing their daily life here and now.

NO "THEORY OF EVERYTHING"

Trotskyists should realise that young "anarchists" are not looking for an all-explaining science as Trotskyists are.

They have a spontaneous distrust of "Marxist-Leninist" Stalinism (which is a rather good thing), but they also think Marx, Lenin and Trotsky are boring guys who lived 70, 100 or 150 years ago and can't deal with today's realities. They obviously hate Lenin and Trotsky for Kronstadt, the repression of anarchists in Russia, etc., but more than everything they are not, unlike Trotskyists, looking for a coherent, scientific point of view. They are inspired by different, heterogeneous, ideas, which seem to Marxists totally incoherent and sometimes even reactionary.

They can be inspired by postmodern or confused multiculturalist intellectuals, as well as by obscure vegan or pre-ecologist thinkers. But you can often be fooled because when they write about "economy" (which every Marxist knows is not a separate reality but interlinked with human social relations), they often use a vague Marxist vocabulary which may lead you to think they are easy to "win" to your beloved Marxist "science". This is a total illusion.

Generally, the anarchist press places much more value on "anecdotes" about daily life and small-scale experiences than most Trotskyist newspapers. Young anarchists value more creative forms of propaganda: street theater, videos on the internet, and large cultural events, which they think are as effective as traditional meetings, newspapers, or leaflets. This is linked with the tradition of the "ateneos" (sorts of cultural centers/libraries, etc.) in the Spanish CNT.

CONCRETE RESULTS

Trotskyists should realise young "anarchists" want to be active in their own milieu — their own community, their own housing estate, their own workplace — and see concrete results of their action now.

That means they don't give a damn about selling papers or distributing leaflets if it is not linked to a concrete change in people's lives. It means that they don't fancy going miles away from their home to distribute leaflets to people they have never met. Or if they do go far away, it's much more to learn about unknown realities than to propagate a specific ideology to supposedly ignorant workers, peasants or oppressed people.

What they do and propose, even on the basis of confused slogans and politics, resonates among young precarious workers or students, influenced by the anti-globalisation movement ideology (the "indignados" is a good example) and they are like a fish in water in these social movements because they don't want to impose an ideology.

MILITANCY AT WORK?

Trotskyists should also know that young anarchists have a different view of militancy at work.Trotskyists have traditionally tried to get jobs in big factories or other large workplaces, and they have occasionally succeeded in getting positions inside the trade union bureaucracy in the public sector (or, less often, in the private sector).

Young anarchists are often very precarious (as all the members of their generation), working in call centres and temporary jobs. That may explain why they are not interested in long-term strategies for building tendencies inside trade unions or in trade union routine, and are much more in direct action in their community more than at their workplace, which is always changing. There also some anarchists (not all of them of course, because some anarchists share Trotskyist tactics of infiltrating the trade union bureaucracy) who think that trade unions represent barriers and brakes on forms of self-organisation among workers, and in many cases are overtly hostile to any autonomous currents that have emerged among radical workers.

This little article may give you the impression that young "anarchists " are hot-blooded, hyper-sensitive, empathetic and funny individuals, while Trotskyists are cold-blooded, insensitive, indifferent and boring persons. There is a bit of truth in both of these mutually shared clichés.

So if Trotskyists want to discuss seriously with today's young anarchists they (as well as their organisations) should start by questioning themselves, along the lines I have just described. Who knows — something interesting may happen.

Anarchism without trade unions: fresh wave or utopianism? A reply to Yves Coleman

By Ira Berkovic

Solidarity 227, 1 December 2011

URL: bit.ly/sPML1W

Yves Coleman's article in *Solidarity* 224 ("Five things Trotskyists Should Know About Today's Young 'Anarchists'") is a little difficult to get to grips with, much the like the politics of the people — "today's young 'anarchists'" — whose corner Yves has chosen to fight. The mirroring of content and form is a neat trick, but it doesn't make a fruitful exchange particularly easy.

Yves objects to a recent series of articles (presumably Martin Thomas's review of Lucien Van Der Walt and Michael Schmidt's book *Black Flame: The Revolutionary Class Politics of Anarchism and Syndicalism*), which he found "too much centred on 'old-style' 19th-century anarchism and not on today's diverse, confused libertarian and anarchist currents." As a point-of-departure, this is a little unfair; the series was a critical review of a recently-published book about the "anarchist tradition" which was recommended by an anarchist in debate with us as the best statement of anarchist views. The series did not pretend to be a comprehensive engagement with all of today's currents. If Yves's objection is that we have not devoted sufficient time to attempting such an engagement, I can only suggest that he takes another look at our recent work and written material. He might try, just for starters, Ed Maltby's "How to organise to change the world" [1] Bob Sutton on the dissolution of Climate Camp [2], or my own "Open letter to a direct-action militant" [3] or "Can we build a revolutionary workers' movement?" [4]. He should note our work in building up networks like No Sweat, Workers' Climate Action and Feminist Fightback — direct-action, activist coordinations that attempted to unite Trotskyists, anarchists and others to organise on the basis of shared class-struggle politics within wider anti-capitalist milieus. Perhaps Yves considers these efforts inadequate or politically misguided, but to suggest that we only engage with anarchists as if they were all nothing more than slavish acolytes of Bakunin and Proudhon is unreasonable. Unlike other Trotskyist organisations (such as the SWP, whose dreadful recent series on "anarchism" used the term interchangeably and incorrectly with "autonomism"), we have attempted to engage critically with anarchism both in its form as a discrete theoretical tradition and in its more diffuse modern manifestation.

MISPLACED

So Yves's ostensible starting point (merely to chivvy the AWL, without agenda, into an engagement with a different expression of "anarchist" ideas) is at the very least, misplaced.

What's the article's purpose? In a correspondence reproduced on the anarchist-dominated website LibCom [5], Yves writes: "If you read my conclusion with accurate glasses it seems clear (at least to me) that if Trotskyists want to discuss with anarchists they should question … their program and leave Trotskyism in the 'dustbins of history'". I have no problem with Yves attempting to persuade us to break with Trotskyism, but if this is his aim he should be upfront about it. I know Yves is committed to real debate — non-sectarian but sharp and serious. Despite his warm words for young anarchists uninterested in old texts, he has given much of his own energy in recent years to digging out and publishing... old texts of anarchism and Marxism. He should write, therefore, so that we can debate the words on the page without "glasses" — "accurate" or otherwise.

I agree that there are specific politics and general ways-of-thinking that have become incorporated into "Trotskyist" common-sense (most of them inherited wholesale from Stalinism) that do belong in "the dustbin of history".

But exactly what specific ideas Yves thinks we should throw out, and what ideas from anarchist traditions — if any — we should replace them with remains a mystery. He doesn't spell it out in his article (or maybe I'm just not wearing the right "glasses").

He is not even clear about whether he agrees with the politics of "today's young anarchists", whose defender and advocate he has apparently appointed himself. On the topic of "militancy at work", for example, Yves argues that "young anarchists" are more interested in "direct action in their community" rather than the workplace. The implication is that precariousness has shifted the nuclear core at which capitalism can be challenged away from struggles in workplaces and the organisations that grow out of them (that is, unions). Yves's describes a "Trotskyist" strategy of "infiltrating the trade union bureaucracy" (appearing to denote by this, not just activities oriented to positions in the official machine, like say the SP's in PCS, but any systematic engagement with trade-union organisation) and says some anarchists share it, but highlights the fact that many anarchists maintain an overt hostility to established labour movements. Certainly, some anarchists do think this. *But are they right to think it?* Does the proliferation of precarious work (call centres, service and retail sector jobs etc.), particularly amongst young people, somehow alter the fundamental analysis that sees the wage relation, in workplaces, specifically (rather than what some anarchists mystically describe as "hierarchy" or "power relations", pervading diffusely throughout all of society and no more or less hegemonic in the workplace than in a classroom or on a housing estate) as the nuclear core of capitalism? We believe that it doesn't. Certainly, the "shape" of the working class has changed since the 60s, 70s and 80s but the essential DNA of capitalism has not.

On the question of "direct action", to give another example, the debate is not whether we should organise it "now" (which the anarchists want, apparently), or reject it until we achieve a "primitive accumulation of militants (or cadres) to build the party": we can all agree that "direct action now" is necessary. The questions are *what kind of direct action, by whom, and for what?*. Yves's article doesn't scratch the surface of those fundamental questions, and is rather poorer for it.

Part of Yves's problem is that, in attempting to speak on behalf of a milieu that is, by definition and by his own admission, diffuse, contradictory and "confused", he can only deal in impressionistic brush-strokes. The politics of the people Yves is attempting to describe are not fixed. They are on a journey — some towards more theoretically-concrete "classical anarchism", some towards anarcho-syndicalism, some perhaps towards the revolutionary syndicalism which bears a great deal in common with our own politics, some away from working-class anti-capitalism altogether and towards individualist lifestylist utopianism. When the AWL meets people at various stages of that political journey, we attempt to engage with them, and not by throwing critiques of Bakunin at them but by trying to identify shared politics to organise around. That common organisation sometimes involves us learning from them, but it also involves identifying where we think they're wrong and attempting to persuade them of our ideas. It is on that terrain, on the terrain of which ideas are right and which are wrong, that the engagement between "Trotskyists" and "today's young 'anarchists'" must take place. The fact that, according to Yves, some "young anarchists […] are not looking for a coherent, scientific point of view" doesn't change this; it simply means that that, too, is an, idea which needs debating.

UTOPIANISM

Many of the ideas Yves describes — a focus on building cooperatives or social centres, an emphasis on organising "non-traditional" groups of workers, a perspective that sees squatting a building as equally anti-capitalist/revolutionary as organising a strike — are modern echoes of pre-Marxist utopian socialism.

You can see them, alive and well, in the Occupy movement, many of whose activists see the establishment and maintenance of the protest camps as an end in itself rather than a symbolic act or an action designed to provide leverage to win political demands (as per the epigraph on Yves's article — "when I cook for the Occupy movement, I contribute to changing the world".) 21st century utopians (which would perhaps be a better label than "anarchists" for the people Yves is describing, although anarchism has always had utopian elements) start from an opposition to capitalism, but often without a clear analysis of what it is or how it works, and a vague idea of an alternative, but without an identifiable agency for achieving it.

The AWL believes that capitalism is not simply an accumulation of its symptoms or bad effects, but a specific system predicated fundamentally on the exploitation of wage labour. It can only be disrupted and overthrown by subverting that exploitative relationship. This means that workers' self-organisation, at the point of exploitation, is "privileged" as a form of organisation. It means that strikes, sit-ins and other forms of class-struggle direct action are "privileged" as forms of action. It means that the organisations organically generated from capitalist class relations (trade unions) are key sites of struggle, no matter how bureaucratic or badly-led they may be. And it means that only workers' self-organisation and struggle can provide a basis for building a new society.

"Today's young 'anarchists'" — our 21st century utopians — don't agree, Yves tells us. Fine. But, to be perhaps a little blunter than Yves would like, they are wrong. The Marxist critique of such perspectives is as valid now as it was in 1848, and is one aspect of our tradition that we are not prepared to junk.

If Yves wants to contribute more productively to a continuing engagement between the AWL and anarchists of whatever stripe and school, he would do better to say precisely which ideas he believes are right and which wrong, rather than setting himself up as an ostensibly-neutral (but in fact partisan) conduit for the constantly-shifting ideas of a layer of activists with which we already have a long experience of engaging.

Enough with the glasses, Yves; let's have the debate in plain view.

[1] bit.ly / f4BVZB
[2] bit.ly / vJ94hW
[3] bit.ly / h0lHYN
[4] bit.ly / jc97HE
[5] bit.ly / vZIFXv

The above references, excluding [5], are also included in this book.